Latino Representation in State Houses and Congress

This book argues that Latino representation in U.S. legislative institutions is shaped not only by demographics, but also by legislative institutional design, as well as elite-driven methods, features of the electoral system, and the increasing mainstreaming of Latinos in American society. The election of Latino legislators in the United States is thus complex and varied. This book provides evidence on how successful Latinos have been in winning state legislative and congressional districts in which they have no natural advantage. In particular, this book demonstrates that Latino candidates benefit from higher percentages of Latino citizens in the state, more liberal citizenries, and citizen legislatures. Jason P. Casellas argues that the legislatures most conducive to the election of Latino candidates are Florida, New Mexico, and California, whereas the least conducive are the U.S. House and New York.

Jason P. Casellas is Assistant Professor of Government and Associate Director of the Irma Rangel Public Policy Institute at the University of Texas at Austin. He specializes in American politics, with specific research and teaching interests in Latino politics, legislative politics, and state and local politics. He is the recipient of numerous fellowships, including a Princeton President's Fellowship, an American Political Science Association Fellowship, and a Ford Motor Company Fellowship. His dissertation won third place in a nationwide interdisciplinary competition for the best dissertation given by the American Association of Hispanics in Higher Education and the Educational Testing Service. In 2007–2008, he was the Samuel DuBois Cook Postdoctoral Fellow at Duke University. In 2009–2010, he was a visiting postdoctoral Fellow at the United States Studies Centre in Sydney, Australia. His work has appeared in the *Journal of Politics*, *Legislative Studies Quarterly*, *Political Research Quarterly*, *Qualitative Methods*, and the *Journal of California Politics and Policy*.

Latino Representation in State Houses and Congress

JASON P. CASELLAS
University of Texas, Austin

CAMBRIDGE
UNIVERSITY PRESS

CAMBRIDGE UNIVERSITY PRESS
Cambridge, New York, Melbourne, Madrid, Cape Town, Singapore,
São Paulo, Delhi, Dubai, Tokyo, Mexico City

Cambridge University Press
32 Avenue of the Americas, New York, NY 10013-2473, USA

www.cambridge.org
Information on this title: www.cambridge.org/9780521198974

© Jason P. Casellas 2011

First published 2011

Printed in the United States of America

A catalog record for this publication is available from the British Library.

Library of Congress Cataloging in Publication data
Casellas, Jason Paul, 1977–
    Latino representation in state houses and Congress / Jason P. Casellas.
       p.   cm.
    Includes bibliographical references and index.
    ISBN 978-0-521-19897-4 (hardback)
    1. Legislative bodies – United States.   2. Legislative bodies – United
    States – States.   3. United States. Congress.   4. Hispanic American
    legislators.   5. Hispanic Americans – Politics and government.   I. Title.
    JK2495.C37   2011
    328.730089'68–dc22   2010031213

ISBN 978-0-521-19897-4 Hardback

To my parents

Contents

Contents

Tables

Figures

Acknowledgments

Words cannot express my appreciation to the many people who have given me the encouragement, advice, and invaluable criticisms that have shaped this book. First and foremost, I am most indebted to my dissertation advisor, R. Douglas Arnold, for always being supportive of my work and helping me become a better scholar and writer. His numerous and always detailed critiques of my drafts have undoubtedly made this book much better than it otherwise would have been. I have always been amazed by Doug's ability to provide timely and, more importantly, quality reactions to my work. This never ceased during my time at Princeton despite a challenge to Doug's health. Secondly, Tali Mendelberg has been a strong supporter of my project ever since we first talked about it in her office early on during my graduate career. Tali has had faith in my abilities since she first read my application file in 2000, and she has continued her support of my work and provided important feedback despite her taking on important departmental responsibilities as Director of Graduate Studies. Her detailed and incisive commentaries on my work no doubt have made this book much clearer and systematic. I am forever indebted to Tali for her valuable mentorship. Larry Bartels has also served as an important advisor, especially in regards to questions I have had regarding the quantitative aspects of my book. Larry's knowledge of redistricting, especially in New Jersey, helped inform my book. I am also indebted to other members of the Princeton faculty, including those in attendance at the American Politics Research Seminar where I presented drafts of this project. The staff at CSDP, including Helene Wood and Diane Price, provided years of support, laughter, and surrogate motherly care during my years in graduate school. Monica Selinger at Princeton made my life a breeze by always looking out for me and enduring my long conversations in her office about topics ranging from where to go in Italy to the ins and outs of navigating the Princeton bureaucracy. I also thank Princeton University's Graduate School, especially Dean David Redman and Danielle Gray, for having confidence in me and asking me to represent the school at various recruiting fairs across the country as a Student Diversity Assistant. I would also like to thank the Horowitz Foundation for Social Policy for a dissertation research grant, which made some of the research presented possible, as well as the Earhart Foundation and Robby George for supplemental financial support during my years at Princeton. Finally, I would also thank John Darley and the Fellowship of Woodrow Wilson Scholars at Princeton University that provided much needed financial and intellectual support at the most critical time of my dissertation writing. Although I organized and collected most of the data used in this project, I thank NALEO, the Secretaries of State for the seven states of my study, David Lublin, and Gary Moncrief for providing important data. I especially thank Nolan McCarty for generously providing state NOMINATE data for the Colorado, New Jersey, and Texas legislatures. I also thank my colleagues at the University of Texas at Austin, for their support and confidence in my abilities, especially John Higley and Gary Freeman, who as chairs of the department have supported my research in many ways. I also thank the University of Texas at Austin Graduate Studies program for generously providing a Summer Research Assignment in 2007, which assisted me in completing a great deal of the research in this book. David Leal has also served as an invaluable mentor to me as a young assistant professor. His leadership of the Public Policy Institute has made my job as the Associate Director flawless and, most important of all, painless. Daron Shaw, Bat Sparrow, and, more recently, Nick Valentino have been wonderful colleagues at UT. I also thank my other faculty colleagues at UT, including Brian Roberts, Tasha Philpot, Eric McDaniel, Ismail White, Corrine McConnaughy, Pat McDonald, Jason Brownlee, Ken Greene, Sean Theriault, and Andy Karch. I especially thank Paula McClain, Kerry Haynie, Mike Munger, John Aldrich, Alisa Kessel, Efren Perez, Niambi Carter, Dick Engstrom, and Mary Bogues for making my time at Duke University's Social Science Research Institute as the first Samuel DuBois Cook Postdoctoral Fellow a valuable and rewarding experience. In particular, I thank Rodney Hero and David Lublin for participating in a Book Manuscript Conference at UT, where they provided excellent feedback on this project. I am also grateful to the U.S. Studies Centre at the University of Sydney, including

Margaret Levi,Geoff Garrett, and Brendon O'Connor, where I completed some of the last-minute edits to this book. I also thank the many anonymous reviewers for providing valuable feedback. Most of all, I thank my family and friends and their prayers for helping me through graduate school and my first few years as an assistant professor. Without them, I could not have survived.

Introduction

In recent political campaigns, candidates have adopted Spanish-language appeals in their efforts to woo the growing Latino vote. The reasons for such appeals are obvious: Latinos are the largest minority group in the United States, and the Pew Hispanic Center estimates that the Latino population will increase from 14 percent of the population in 2007 to nearly 30 percent of the population in 2050.[1] However, although the growth of Latinos in American legislative institutions has slowly increased in the past decade, Latinos remain underrepresented in Congress and state legislatures. Even though Congress has long been the focal point for studies of representation, a comparative analysis of Congress and state legislatures has yet to be done. This book is the first systematic examination of the election of Latinos to U.S. state legislatures and Congress.

This book argues that Latino representation is dependent on subethnic diversity, distinct political backgrounds even among Mexican Americans, and nascent political experience. The central argument is that Latino representation in U.S. legislative institutions is shaped not only by demographics, but also by legislative institutional design, as well as elite-driven methods, features of the electoral system, and the increasing mainstreaming of Latinos in American society. The election of Latino legislators in the United States is thus complex and varied.

Through specifying the political processes and mechanisms of Latino political incorporation, the central questions this book addresses are as follows: How do we explain the election of Latino candidates to Congress

---

[1] See the Pew Hispanic Center website for reports on the growing Latino population in the United States (http://www.pewhispanic.org).

and state legislatures? Do Latino candidates have unique obstacles being elected to legislative office? To what extent have Latinos benefited from the creation of majority-Latino districts in order to be elected? Are Latinos a special group or just another of the many ethnic groups in the American melting pot? Are Latino candidates as advantaged when they run in districts filled with citizens who share their ethnic heritage as other ethnic candidates have been throughout American history? Are they seriously disadvantaged when they run in heterogeneous districts? How do Latino representatives see themselves? What difference does it make whether Latino legislators represent Latinos? Do Latino representatives behave differently than non-Latino representatives? This book provides answers to all of these questions.

Why are these questions important in the first place? Especially since the Voting Rights Act of 1965, scholars, pundits, and political observers have debated issues regarding race, redistricting, and legislative representation. For example, the Supreme Court weighed in on the Voting Rights Act in a 2009 ruling that overturned a lower court's decision to require an Austin, Texas utility district to comply with Section 5 of the Act, which requires the Department of Justice to "preclear" any changes in voting procedures. Chief Justice John Roberts wrote that Section 5 "raises serious constitutional concerns" that can only be justified by "current needs" rather than the legacy of racial discrimination.[2] This book provides evidence to show how successful Latinos have been in winning state legislative and congressional districts in which they have no natural advantage. In particular, across seven diverse states and Congress, this book demonstrates the institutional and demographic determinants of Latino representation, as well as the extent to which Latino legislators see themselves as distinctive representatives.

These questions are also especially important as the number of Latinos in American society continues to grow every day. Latinos currently constitute 14 percent of American society, and this percentage is estimated to reach 18 percent by 2025.[3] Should we expect that the flow of Latino candidates into Congress and state legislatures will increase at comparable levels as Latino citizens increase in numbers and put down their

---

[2] Qtd. In *The Economist,* June 27, 2009.
[3] The number of Latinos in the United States reached 44.3 million on July 1, 2006, accounting for about one-half of people added to the nation's population since July 1, 2005. These estimates do not include the island of Puerto Rico (from U.S. Census American Fact Finder).

political roots? Or to what extent does the election of Latino candidates rest on governments drawing legislative districts that favor their election? Although these questions are important, they are not the ones scholars have investigated thoroughly.

The second reason that questions about Latino representation are important is that they reflect underlying questions about race and ethnicity broadly conceived. Some people assume that the story of Latino candidates parallels the story of African-American candidates. According to this view, the only way to increase the number of Latino legislators is to create districts with Latino majorities. Although majority-African-American districts were apparently necessary for the election of substantial numbers of African-American legislators, there are reasons to believe that the story might not be quite the same for Latino candidates. First, many Latinos have not suffered centuries of discrimination.[4] Whatever discrimination Latino citizens suffer is probably somewhere between that of other volunteer immigrants – for example, Irish, Italian, and Polish Americans – and the discrimination imposed on people brought to the country in chains (Erie 1988; Skerry 1993). Second, Latino citizens have more choices than do African-American citizens about whether to identify strongly with their heritage or to hide it by diving into the melting pot. Ethnic self-identity is often a choice; skin color is not. As Dawson (1994) and Pinderhughes (1987) show, African Americans have experienced difficulties regarding political incorporation precisely because of this history of American racism based on skin color. Likewise, Massey and Denton (1993) make clear that individuals with black skin color face more discrimination than Latinos and Asians. At the same time, there is no question that Latinos have experienced discrimination in many ways (Hero 1992; Montejano 1999).

This book goes beyond previous studies of Latino representation, which only focus on Congress. Such an analysis offers significant advantages. First, it expands the number of Latino politicians to be studied. Because only twenty-eight Latinos currently serve in Congress, focusing exclusively on how those politicians gained office does not provide much leverage on the central questions. Approximately 220 Latinos serve in the fifty state legislatures, which provides a larger pool of subjects. Second, broadening the study to include state legislators increases the variance

---

[4] This does not suggest that Latinos have not suffered discrimination. In particular, stories abound about discrimination in the Southwest and even South Florida where real estate signs compared Mexicans and Cubans to dogs.

in the explanatory variables. Some states have high concentrations of Latinos; most do not. Some states have been more aggressive than have others in creating majority-Latino districts. Some states elect two or more legislators from the same districts. This increased variance makes it easier to assess the impact of demographic patterns, districting arrangements, and electoral laws on the election of Latino candidates. Third, serving as a state legislator often provides a stepping-stone toward congressional election. Women were not elected to Congress in large numbers until they first succeeded in state legislatures. Examining Latino representation in state legislatures offers a window on the future of Latinos in Congress. Finally, state legislatures are themselves important. One cannot understand domestic policy making without appreciating the role of state governments and state legislatures.

Latinos in American Society

Latinos are the fastest-growing minority group in the United States and have surpassed African Americans as the largest minority group in the country. Latinos are also a diverse group. They differ markedly in their geographic origins, their length of residence, and their identification with being Latino. Many Mexican Americans, for example, have resided in the Southwest for hundreds of years. Their unique cultural history is part of the political culture in states such as Texas, California, or New Mexico. Most Puerto Rican and Cuban immigrants, however, have more recently immigrated to the mainland United States for economic and political reasons, respectively. For many years, the Census merely collected data on those with "Spanish surnames," but today, the Census collects data on country of origin. It was not until the 1960s that the number of Latino immigrants swelled, making the United States the fifth-largest Spanish-speaking country in the world.

Unlike African Americans, Latinos are less reliably tied to the Democrats. Although only 20 percent of Latinos nationwide are registered Republican, President George W. Bush received approximately 35 percent of the Latino vote in the 2000 election. Foreign-born Latinos, second-generation Latinos, and third-generation Latinos classify themselves somewhat differently. The longer a Latina is in the United States, the more likely she is to be a Democrat. Foreign-born Latinos are the most likely to identify themselves as Independent, which helps explain why political campaigns have used Spanish-language advertising in many battleground states. Fourteen percent of third-generation Latinos call themselves Republicans, whereas a statistically indistinguishable 11 percent of foreign-born Latinos call themselves Republican. Since approximately 35 percent of Latinos are independent, both political parties have recently campaigned for their support. A closer look at the history of Mexican Americans, Puerto Rican Americans, and Cuban Americans illustrates the sociological and political diversity of Latinos.

Mexican Americans

Mexican Americans are the largest and oldest Latino group in the United States and comprise the majority of Latino legislators. More than two-thirds of Latinos living in the United States are Mexican American. Much of the Southwest was part of Mexico until the Treaty of Guadalupe Hidalgo in 1848 (Gann and Duignan 1986: 17). This treaty ceded territory that eventually became eight states. Many Mexicans lived on this land and remained even after control switched from Mexico to the United States. Once non-Latino Americans settled in these territories, racial friction and prejudice emerged. Many Americans viewed Mexicans as "cowardly, ignorant, lazy, and addicted to gambling and alcohol" (Gann and Duignan 1986: 14).

Mexican Americans currently represent one-quarter of the electorate in such crucial states as Texas and California. Mexican Americans have traditionally been loyal members of the Democratic Party, although in places like New Mexico, Republicans have long worked to incorporate Latinos into their fold. In New Mexico, approximately 16 percent of Latinos are registered Republicans. The number of "not so strong Democrats" nationwide is nearly 30 percent for Mexican Americans, more so than any other Latino group. Mexican Americans are more likely to vote for Democratic candidates than Republicans but are not as strong in their support of the Democratic Party as Cuban Americans are of the Republican Party.[5]

Not only are Mexican Americans the oldest and most established Latino group in the United States, but they are also the fastest-growing Latino group. Whereas most Mexican Americans originally settled in California and the Southwest, recent waves of Mexican immigrants have settled all across the United States, especially in the Midwest and South. In fact, the Tomás Rivera Policy Institute reports that nine of the top

---

[5] See Latino National Survey (2008) for further details on Latino voter attitudes.

ten fastest-growing Latino counties in the United States are in the states of Arkansas, Georgia, and North Carolina.[6] The growth of Mexican migrant workers is not limited to the South, either. Even industrial areas in the Midwest have experienced a rapid growth of Mexican workers in recent years.

Puerto Rican Americans

Puerto Ricans are unique among Latinos. They are United States citizens whether they reside in Puerto Rico or settle in any of the fifty states. Unlike other Latinos, they are never "illegal" immigrants. Puerto Ricans comprise about 9 percent of the United States Latino population, and most of them have traditionally settled in New York City. Puerto Ricans first migrated to New York following the Spanish American War. It was not until after World War II that Puerto Ricans migrated en masse to New York (Gann and Duignan 1986: 78). Puerto Rican immigration to the United States has been attributed to "the economic policies of the United States and the island's government, which have encouraged industrialization and capitalist investment" (Hero 1992: 39). Like today's Mexican immigrants, Puerto Ricans have come to the mainland United States for economic improvement and prosperity. More recently, however, Puerto Ricans have increasingly chosen central Florida as a preferred destination. According to the Puerto Rican Federal Affairs Administration, nearly 650,000 Puerto Ricans reside in Florida. In 2002, then-Governor Jeb Bush won 55 percent of the non-Cuban Latino vote (which includes a large portion of Puerto Ricans), according to Democratic pollster Sergio Bendixen.

Despite the more partisan split in Florida among Puerto Ricans, most have nonetheless been strong supporters of the Democratic Party, and major Puerto Rican members of Congress have been strong Democrats. Approximately 50 percent of Puerto Ricans are registered Democrats.[7] Puerto Ricans tend to support increased government support for the poor and see the Democratic Party as more willing to care and implement programs designed to help the economically disadvantaged. In recent elections, Puerto Ricans have supported Democratic candidates in large numbers. In 1996, former President Clinton captured 93 percent of the Puerto Rican vote. Nevertheless, some Republican candidates have found

---

[6] See Tomás Rivera Policy Institute website for precise numbers (http://www.trpi.org).

[7] See Pew Hispanic Center/Kaiser Foundation National Survey of Latinos: The Latino Electorate, 2002 (http://www.pewhispanic.org/site/docs/pdf/latino_chartpack_092002.pdf).

ways to appeal to Puerto Rican voters. Former Mayor Rudolph Giuliani (R-New York) captured 37 percent of the Puerto Rican vote in his successful mayoral re-election campaign. Mayor Michael R. Bloomberg (I-New York) won his 2001 race with strong support from New York City's Latino community, which is mostly Puerto Rican and Dominican. Dominicans have consistently supported the mayor at higher levels than Puerto Ricans, though. Bloomberg was also perceptive in appealing to Dominicans, who are the fastest-growing immigrant group in parts of New York City (e.g., The Bronx). One could argue that these numbers merely indicate the failure of the Republicans at the national level and the success of Giuliani and Bloomberg at the local level. The better lesson is that Puerto Ricans are not "Yellow Dog" Democrats: They respond to candidate appeals, not only to party loyalty.

Cuban Americans

Most Cuban Americans came to the United States following Fidel Castro's revolution of 1959. Cuban Americans comprise only 4 percent of the United States Latino population, and the largest number settled in the Miami area. Cuban Americans came to the United States more for political refuge than for economic opportunities. Gann and Duignan note that "when many Mexican or Puerto Rican intellectuals turned to anti-establishment politics in the United States, most Cubans looked upon the United States as a refuge against tyranny" (1986, 110).

This distinction is crucial when determining why most Cuban Americans vote Republican and why most Cuban members of Congress and state legislators are also Republican. Traditionally, the Republican Party has been more supportive than the Democratic Party of tightening the trade embargo on Cuba. In addition, many Cuban Americans perceived the Republican Party as more anticommunist during the Cold War. More than two-thirds of Cuban Americans oppose U.S. relations with Cuba. Forty-eight percent of Cubans surveyed classified themselves as strong Republicans. This figure exceeds the number of Puerto Ricans and Mexican Americans who claim to be strong Democrats by approximately ten percentage points and sixteen percentage points, respectively.[8] In addition, Cuban Americans born in Cuba during the Castro years are less likely to be Republican because they were not subjected to the discourse of "el exilio" in heavily Republican Miami. Cuban Americans who

---

[8] See Pew Hispanic Center/Kaiser Foundation National Survey of Latinos: The Latino Electorate, 2002 (http://www.pewhispanic.org/site/docs/pdf/latino_chartpack_092002.pdf).

speak at least some Spanish are more likely to be Republican, especially those who were born in Cuba. This has to do with the large number of Cuban-born exiles who left Cuba in 1980 during the Mariel boatlift, whose political attitudes are not as hardline as those who left immediately following the revolution. It appears then that immigrants who left Cuba after 1959 but before the Mariel boatlift in 1980 are more likely to identify as partisan Republicans.

In 2000, the Elián González controversy ignited the passions of many Cuban Americans and their congressional representatives who believed that the Clinton Administration's Department of Justice, headed by Janet Reno, improperly sent the young boy back to an oppressive tyrannical regime. Many Cuban Americans who themselves left behind mothers, fathers, and siblings in Cuba in the early 1960s saw this incident as an affront to the principle that the ability to live in freedom easily outweighs the rights of a father. Al Gore broke with President Clinton and believed that the boy should have been allowed to stay in the United States. Despite this position, Gore received fewer Cuban American votes in Florida in 2000 than did Clinton in 1996, thus costing him Florida's crucial electoral votes. In 2004, President Bush won the state of Florida in the general election by a comfortable margin. The presence of a Cuban American, Mel Martínez, in the U.S. Senate race had a reverse coattail effect by which Cuban American voters turned out in large numbers for the Republican ticket. Overall, Bush received 54 percent of the Latino vote, whereas Martínez received 59 percent of the Latino vote in Florida. Among Cuban Americans, Bush and Martínez enjoyed over 80 percent of the vote, according to CNN exit polls. In Florida, Cuban Americans are an influential voting bloc, even though other Latino groups comprise the majority of the Latino population.[9]

This brief history is by no means exhaustive, but when I refer to "subethnic" differences throughout the book, I am referring to differences among the three major Latino groups. Because Mexican Americans, Puerto Ricans, and Cuban Americans are often lumped together as "Latinos," it behooves us to think carefully about context, region, skin color, and historical background within and across the group.

---

[9] According to the U.S. Census, Cuban Americans account for 5 percent of the population in Florida. Latinos as a whole comprise 16 percent of the population. Other Latino groups comprise 6 percent of the entire state population, whereas Puerto Ricans comprise 3 percent and Mexican Americans 2 percent.

Latino Political Incorporation

What is the best theoretical way to understand Latino political incorporation? Moreover, at what point does a mainstream entrance into the political process replace ethnic-based politics? Early scholars such as Dahl (1961) argued that ethnic minorities initially are bound together by common characteristics and coalesce for political action, often by party elites eager to bring in more voters. In New Haven, the newer Italian American immigrants were courted by the Republican Party in opposition to the Irish-controlled Democratic Party. In a similar way, some Republicans have tried to court Latinos away from the Democratic Party, which has been the party most Latinos identify with.

In the past several presidential elections, both political parties began appealing to Latino voters through Spanish-language media and targeted outreach efforts. As a result, more and more Latinos feel empowered to the point of having a stake in the political process (Rogers 2006). The questions then become: Are Latinos beginning to shed their ethnic loyalties and think of themselves as American? And do non-Latinos begin to see Latinos as American? As this transformation develops, we will presumably begin to see more Latinos elected to office from districts with non-Latino majorities.

The process of assimilation often develops over the course of two generations, as many sociologists have observed (Alba and Nee 2003). To what extent will Latinos follow the path of Europe's ethnic immigrants or the more difficult incorporation of African Americans? As Dawson (1994) has shown, the pluralist model does not account for racial discrimination and prejudice. African Americans still suffer disproportionately from poverty and other social ailments, just as many Latino groups do. Accordingly, Hero (1992) articulated a theory of "two-tiered pluralism" to explain the Latino experience in America, which acknowledges the history of discrimination and subordination but contends that pluralism best explains Latino political incorporation (although not as successful as for white ethnics). As we will see with many of the Latino legislators elected to non-Latino majority districts, a "Latino" identity is often not acknowledged or made known to voters. Many of these Latino representatives see themselves as regular Americans representing their districts. Before turning to a more in-depth discussion of Latino representation, it might be useful to review how political scientists have understood the concept.

The Concept of Representation

Empirical scholars in political science have generally allowed normative theorists to conceptualize key concepts such as democracy, accountability, and representation (Collier and Adcock 1999; Pitkin 1967). For some empiricists, taking the time to revisit the very concepts they are purportedly measuring and testing seems at best too philosophical, and hence out of their domain, although Goertz (2006) offers a comprehensive treatment of social science concepts. Consequently, the empirical literature on representation has focused too heavily on statistical roll call analyses, which to a certain degree can help us ascertain the extent to which legislators represent their constituents in legislatures and Congress. Substantive representation, however, involves much more than how legislators vote. In order for political scientists to understand why, we must think carefully about what representation involves in terms of concepts, typologies, and case selection.

Normative Conceptions of Representation

Starting with Pitkin (1967), political scientists have regarded representation as either descriptive or substantive. Descriptive representation refers to citizens being represented by legislators who share particular demographic characteristics (race, gender, or ethnicity), whereas substantive representation involves legislators representing citizens' interests or particular preferences. Scholars of black representation have debated the merits of which type of representation is most effective, with Swain (1993) arguing that substantive representation is what really counts whereas Mansbridge (1999) places more value on descriptive representation. Mansbridge, however, is a normative theorist who has argued that descriptive representation is essential for advancement of minorities and women in the American political system. Pitkin's analysis did not really deal with minority representation, but the concept she presented has been extended to such studies. To date, no work on racial representation has challenged Pitkin's conceptual framework or analyzed the concept of representation using more recent empirical research on methods.[10]

---

[10] This is not the case regarding gender representation. See Celis (2008) for a thorough review of representation from a women's studies perspective.

The Concept(s)

What does it mean to be represented? What does it mean to represent others? We are always asking others to represent us before a lawmaking body, a Court, or other institution. When one is represented by an attorney before a court, the attorney acts in the material interests of her client. It does not matter whether the attorney looks like her client physically. As long as the attorney defends her client well, then the client will be satisfied. In terms of *political* representation, however, surely more is at stake than just material interests. As Aristotle observed long ago, political issues deal with how we ought to order our lives together in the larger community. Additionally, politics deals with how individuals will be treated, including policies such as affirmative action, immigration, and English Only laws, just to name a few. This distinction is crucial because when Pitkin talks about descriptive and substantive representation, she is referring to political representation. As Gerring explains, concepts are not static and "progress in the cultural sciences occurs, if it occurs at all, through changing terms and definitions" (Gerring 2001). Issues of race and representation have dramatically changed since Pitkin's exegesis, which requires conceptual revisions.

All too often, social scientists have viewed variables as independent of each other. With regard to representation, scholars have dichotomized representation by splitting the concept into descriptive and substantive. Scholars such as Charles Ragin would argue for a configuration where these two concepts are placed in a spatial continuum in a way that acknowledges the diversity, albeit limited, of the concept of representation. As Ragin explains, membership in sets is "often partial" and rarely do we find cases that are either in or out of a given category (Ragin 1999).

In the area of representation, most empirical researchers have chosen to use Pitkin's dichotomy to test whether given groups are being adequately represented. For the most part, scholars in this research tradition have argued that substantive representation is what really matters, although many scholars argue that there is intrinsic value in descriptive representation based on issues of justice such that certain groups, especially women, should have some parity in political institutions (Phillips 1995; Young 1997).

These matters are important in that many of the arguments regarding which type of representation matters deal more with conceptualization than with how representation per se is measured. Hardly anyone would disagree that descriptive representation without substantive representation is not worth very much. However, the real question is whether those who represent districts with different demographic characteristics can adequately represent their constituents *despite* the physical difference. In this sense, the scholarship on racial representation suffers because of a lack of attention to the conceptualization of representation.[11]

Typologies

How should representation be conceptualized? The previous section offered a critique of the prevailing norms of research regarding the issue of political representation. Given the complexity of this concept, it is fitting to explore the many different cells that comprise the "property space" of the concept of representation.[12] A typology is a device for "partitioning events into types that share specified combinations of factors" (Stinchcombe 1968). Typologies can be complex or simple. Typologies for democracy can become quite complex, whereas typologies for approval ratings for the President are quite simple. In the area of representation, I am arguing that the prevailing typology is too simple, and that we need to complicate this concept further into a more encompassing typology, much in the same way Elman (2005) has done for the study of international politics.

As discussed in the previous section, Ragin has offered a framework that assesses the importance of typologies and their implications. Ragin rightly points out that many researchers do not know where to proceed once their typology is fleshed out. In the tradition started by Lazarsfeld's property space typology construction, Ragin sets forth his configurational approach as the heir to Lazarsfeld. Through functional reduction, it is argued, researchers can narrow the domain of researchable cells. In the case of racial representation, it is conceivable to imagine various scenarios of elected representatives and their demographic characteristics, such as black, urban, Democratic members from majority-Latino districts, and so on. For example, in Chapter 4, using Mill's methods, I identify the commonalities and differences among Latino legislators elected to represent districts that are not majority-Latino.

Gerring offers insight into precisely how to create a typology for social scientific concepts. In his analysis of ideology, Gerring notes

[11] This is not the case in the literature on gender and representation, where there has been more of an effort to address these important issues. See Phillips (1998), Young (1997), and Celis (2008) for explicit treatments of gender and representation.
[12] See Lazarsfeld and Barton (1951) for more on the issue of property spaces in political science research.

that typologies are usually created in several ways. First, he notes that empirical researchers can appropriate the definition of a classic work on the concept, which in the case of representation has been the case with Pitkin's framework. Second, scholars can adopt a "causal-explanatory" understanding of the concept by which he means that a concept can be described by what explains it. For example, in the case of representation, one can say that to represent and be represented is one of the key aspects of Democratic systems, and thus one can only examine representation in terms of how the represented and the one representing interact (Chapter 5 examines this interaction from the viewpoints of Latino legislators). Gerring proposes a schema that focuses on "specific definitional attributes" of the given concept (Gerring 2001). Researchers should formulate a minimal definition of the concept as well as an ideal-type definition.

Case Selection

Once one performs adequate conceptualization and typology formation, one of the most challenging tasks is to ensure that cases are chosen carefully. Very little agreement exists on how to choose cases.[13] As Gerring (2001) points out, one of the main goals of social science is achieving representativeness in a given sample. That is, one should avoid bias in the cases we choose. With respect to the concept of representation, then, it is crucial to choose cases that are representative of the type of representation we are trying to study. For example, it would be unrepresentative to generalize about Mexican American members of Congress by only selecting Rep. Henry Bonilla (R-Texas) for an interview because he was the only Mexican Republican in Congress at the time and his views are not representative of many Mexican Americans.[14] Gerring suggests that random samples are always solutions to selection bias, but in the case of racial representation in Congress, it would be foolish to pick a random sample of a population of twenty members of Congress. As the methodology section later describes, I have attempted to select Latinos from various backgrounds, subethnic groups, regions, and genders in my interviews. One of the cardinal sins of social science is selection bias.[15] Selection bias

---

[13] Van Evera offers a list of eleven criteria for case selection, with a matrix aimed at making criteria for case selection easier for graduate students writing their dissertations (p. 88).

[14] Please indulge the unfortunate relationship of the concept of representation with representativeness.

[15] See Achen and Snidal (1993) who refer to selection bias as an "inferential felony with devastating implications."

occurs when selection takes place on the dependent variable, thus biasing conclusions in many instances. Because qualitative research is more susceptible to selection bias, special attention must be given to methodology in order to avoid criticism that is often unjustified.

With respect to studies on representation, Richard Fenno's seminal work on members of Congress has formed the basis by which other studies of representation have proceeded. His research design involved carefully selecting cases to ensure regional and political representativeness. He did not merely interview whomever he had the opportunity to interview and observe. He carefully selected subjects based on pre-ordained criteria in order to ensure representativeness (more on how I selected my interviews in Chapter 5). He did not assume that more and more interviews would be the answer to selection bias. Had he only chosen Democrats, his study would have been biased based on party affiliation. To assess whether the representatives are representing the represented, it is important to say a few words about what Latino interests are and how, despite the subethnic differences outlined above, there are nevertheless various policies and opinions that unite Latinos. Therefore, the next section turns to what precisely constitutes a "Latino interest."

Latino Interests

As the previous discussion on subethnic differences reveals, precisely what constitutes a "Latino interest" varies across time and group. Cuban Americans, Mexican Americans, and Puerto Ricans differ in the importance they place on certain issues; however, on a host of issues, all three groups converge in terms of public opinion. For example, all three groups are generally socially conservative and economically liberal. Conventional wisdom suggests that Cuban Americans are more socially conservative than Puerto Ricans, but as numerous public opinion studies have shown, Puerto Ricans are actually more anti-abortion than Cuban Americans (Uhlaner and Garcia 2002). Although the Republican Party has been trying to raise the salience of abortion among Latino communities, neither of the three major groups as a whole has demonstrated a willingness to vote for the Republican Party based on this position. Many evangelical Latinos, however, have voted for Republicans largely based on their social conservatism.

Unlike other Americans, Latinos of all ethnicities generally believe in income redistribution. According to a Pew Hispanic Center and Henry J. Kaiser Family Foundation survey of Latino voters, 58 percent of Latino

Democrats and 52 percent of Latino Republicans would rather pay higher taxes to support a larger government. Only 35 percent of whites and a surprisingly low 43 percent of African Americans would willingly pay higher taxes to support a larger government. English-dominant Latinos are the least likely (52 percent) to support a larger government, whereas Spanish-dominant and bilingual Latinos strongly support a larger government (62 and 63 percent, respectively). Latinos are also more likely than African Americans and whites to believe that Latino immigrants need to learn English to succeed in America (89 percent versus 86 percent for both African Americans and whites).[16]

Latinos are also more concerned about certain sets of issues than other groups in American society. In particular, Latinos identify education, health care, economic security, and crime as more pressing issues than whites or African Americans (Griffin and Newman 2008). Because of these issue concerns, Latino legislators should be expected to emphasize their positions on these issues in their three major activities: advertising, credit claiming, and position taking (Mayhew 1974). Indeed, as later chapters will show, Latino legislators pointed to many of these issue concerns when discussing their roles as legislators.

Brief Discussion of Subsequent Chapters

Chapter 1 introduces the landscape of Latino political representation in the United States, including the historical and theoretical antecedents of this growing demographic. Although some work has focused on the election of Latinos to Congress, little or no attention has been paid to the increasing numbers of Latinos serving in state legislatures. In that chapter, I identify the key arguments in the literature on black, women, and Latino representation and argue that a more nuanced understanding is needed for the study of Latino representation in U.S. legislatures. Namely, the literature has overemphasized roll call voting analyses and ignored the institutional and demographic conditions under which Latinos are elected to legislative bodies. Through an examination of state-level and district-level data, I argue that institutional criteria such as professionalization, term limits, and legislative design have a profound affect on

---

[16] See Pew Hispanic Center/Kaiser Family Foundation *National Survey of Latinos: The Latino Electorate*, October 2002 for more details. Differences with respect to social and foreign policy issues exist within the Latino community, and this survey reveals such divisions.

Latino representation. Moreover, key differences emerge among the key states in terms of the conduciveness of the election of Latinos to certain legislative bodies. Latinos are increasingly getting elected to districts without Latino majorities through a combination of strategic decision making, exploitation of the electoral system, and elite-level assistance. I also make the case that Latino legislators see themselves as distinctive and necessary for the advancement of Latino interests.

Chapter 2 provides a comprehensive look at Latino representation in all fifty states by tracking the growth of Latinos serving in legislatures in the past two decades and specifying the extent to which institutional, political, and ethnic factors contribute to Latino descriptive representation. I estimate the extent to which the percentage turnover in each state legislature, the presence of term limits legislation, lower or upper chamber, the Democratic share of the presidential vote, and the level of professionalization have an effect on Latino representation in state legislatures. At the state level, Latino representation in the legislature is largely reflective of the percentage of Latinos in the population. States with larger proportions of liberal voters are also more likely to have higher levels of Latino representation because of elite-driven ways to ensure it, and because liberal voters are more likely to support Latino candidates, who are disproportionately Democratic. Additionally, some states have much higher turnover rates in their legislatures, thus opening up more seats for talented Latinos to win. Alternatively, Latinos may have better chances of being elected in states that have enacted term limits, which eliminates the incumbency advantage.

Chapter 3 argues that the Latino presence in state legislatures is not merely a result of demographics, but the percentage of Latino citizens in a district, as well as the institutional design of the state legislature, has important, measurable effects on Latino representation. I use statistical analysis based on my collection of state-level legislative data from seven states going back to the 1990s to determine the extent to which the percentage of Latinos and Latino citizens in a district helps explain the presence of Latinos in state legislatures and Congress. I also test the hypothesis that the percentage of African Americans in a district is positively associated with the presence of Latinos in legislatures, as well as the contention that a Latino candidate is more likely to be elected to the lower-level chamber than to the upper chamber.

Chapter 4 explores the various entry opportunities of Latino candidates in non-Latino districts. Using elite interviews and archival research,

I have compiled the first-ever database of all Latino legislators elected to non-Latino majority districts. This chapter identifies patterns that can help explain the election of the sixty-five Latinos who serve nationwide in non-Latino majority districts. First, I identify elite-driven methods, such as redistricting, recruitment by party leaders, and appointments by governors that have helped enhance the descriptive representation of Latinos in non-Latino majority districts. Second, I examine how several features of the electoral system, such as multicandidate primaries and minority primary coalitions, have also contributed to Latino victories in these districts. Finally, I examine the growing number of Latinos with non-Latino names who have won in non-Latino majority districts and determine the extent to which this has contributed to their success.

Chapter 5 argues that Latino legislators see themselves in distinct ways with varying political backgrounds and perceptions of the importance of descriptive representation on substantive representation. I examine how Latino legislators see themselves in terms of political background, their legislative districts, election to current position, political ambition, and their perceptions of representation. This chapter is the culmination of over twenty in-depth, face-to-face interviews with Latino legislators from places as diverse as Florida and Utah. In it, I identify labor unions as common places of early political involvement among Latinos. The chapter also shows that most Latinos identify their districts in racial and class terms, most have considered or are actively considering running for higher office, and most identify different issues, ranging from water rights to stopping gang graffiti in their districts, as highly important to them. As Tip O'Neill once said, "All politics is local." Although this is true for Latino representatives, most Latino representatives nevertheless indicate a sense of linked fate and indicate that being Latino helps them represent their Latino constituents in a way that non-Latinos cannot.

Chapter 6 examines roll call votes in the U.S. House, as well as a select group of state legislatures, to determine if Latino legislators vote differently than their non-Latino counterparts. Through the use of existing Poole-Rosenthal ideology scores, as well as new ideology scores developed for state legislatures, this chapter explores whether having Latinos in high places makes any difference in terms of substantive policy outcomes. Key explanatory variables helping explain ideology include the percentage of Latinos in a district, the percentage of African Americans in a district, whether a district is represented by a Latino, and the political party of the member. While Espino (2003) and Lublin (1997) have examined similar questions, this chapter adds several state legislatures to examine whether the patterns we have seen at the federal level are similar to state-level voting.

Chapter 7 returns to the central questions posed at the start of this chapter and provides an overall assessment of the causes and consequences of having Latino legislators. This chapter also assesses the public policy implications of redistricting and term limits on Latino representation in Congress and state legislatures.

I

Latinos in Legislatures

Historical and Theoretical Setting

Before the Voting Rights Act in 1965, few Latinos served in the U.S. Congress. Before 1912, only one Latino, California Republican Romualdo Pacheco, served in the U.S. House (Vigil 1996). With the exception of New Mexico and Louisiana, no state sent a Latino to Congress between 1912 and 1960 (Lublin 1997). The Congressional Hispanic Caucus began in 1976 through the efforts of Democratic Reps. Herman Badillo (NY), Baltasar Corrada (PR), E. Kika de la Garza (TX), Henry B. González (TX), and Edward Roybal (CA). Compared to the Congressional Black Caucus, the Hispanic caucus is newer and smaller. In 1992 and 1994, African-American representatives numbered thirty-eight whereas Latinos numbered seventeen (Lublin 1997). In 2005, the number of Latinos serving in Congress had increased to twenty-five. More groundbreaking, however, was the election of two Latinos to the U.S. Senate in 2004. By 2008, Sen. Robert Menéndez (D-NJ) was elected to the U.S. Senate, giving Latinos three U.S. senators for the first time in history. Until 2004, no Latino had served in the Senate since New Mexico's Joseph Montoya, who served until 1977.

As shown in Table 1.1 (both parts a and b), the number of Latinos in Congress had increased to twenty-five by 2008. As shown in Table 1.2, the growth of Latinos in Congress is partly a consequence of the national growth in the Latino population. It especially reflects the concentration of Latinos in California, Texas, and Florida, which now send sixteen Latino representatives to the House (seven for California, six for Texas, and three for Florida). The growth of Latinos in Congress can also be attributed to the redistricting process, which created more districts

TABLE I.IA. *Latino Representatives in the U.S. Congress Ranked in Descending Order of Latino Population, 2009*

Name	District	% Latino	% Black	Party
Rubén Hinojosa	15-Texas	78	2	Democrat
Henry Cuellar	28-Texas	78	1	Democrat
Silvestre Reyes	16-Texas	78	3	Democrat
Lucille Roybal-Allard	34-California	77	4	Democrat
Luis V.Gutiérrez	4-Illinois	75	4	Democrat
Grace Napolitano	38-California	71	4	Democrat
Lincoln Díaz –Balart	21-Florida	70	7	Republican
Xavier Becerra	31-California	70	4	Democrat
Solomon Ortíz	27-Texas	68	3	Democrat
Charles González	20-Texas	67	7	Democrat
Loretta Sánchez	47-California	65	2	Democrat
Ciro Rodríguez	23-Texas	65	3	Democrat
José Serrano	16-New York	63	36	Democrat
Ed Pastor	2-Arizona	63	5	Democrat
Ileana Ros-Lehtinen	18-Florida	63	6	Republican
Mario Díaz-Balart	25-Florida	62	10	Republican
Hilda Solís	32-California	62	3	Democrat
Linda Sánchez	39-California	61	6	Democrat
Joe Baca	43-California	58	3	Democrat
Raúl Grijalva	7-Arizona	51	3	Democrat
Nydia Velázquez	12-New York	49	9	Democrat
Albio Sires	13-New Jersey	48	11	Democrat
John Salazar	3-Colorado	22	1	Democrat
Bob Menéndez	Sen-New Jersey	13	13	Democrat

Source: National Journal's *Almanac of American Politics*, 2009.

with significant numbers of Latinos.[1] The National Association of Latino Elected and Appointed Officials (NALEO) estimates that 122 (28 percent) of the 435 U.S. House districts have Latino populations that surpass the national average.[2] The Southwest and California clearly have the highest percentages, but Latinos have surpassed African Americans as the largest minority group in other states, including New Jersey and New York. This book will explore in more detail the determinants of the growth in the number of Latinos serving in Congress and many state legislatures.

[1] Ex-Rep. Bob Menéndez (D-NJ) won his seat in 1992, following redistricting, whereas Rep. Mario Díaz-Balart (R-FL) won his seat in 2002 following redistricting.
[2] Obtained from NALEO Election Guide, published and available at http://www.naleo. org, 2008.

TABLE 1.1B. *Non-Latino Representatives in the U.S. Congress Ranked in Descending Order of Latino Population (40 Percent and Above Districts), 2009*

Name	District	% Latino	% Black	Party
Gene Green	29th District-TX	66.1	9.7	Democrat
Jim Costa	20th District-CA	63.1	7.2	Democrat
Howard Berman	28th District-CA	55.6	4.1	Democrat
Bob Filner	51st District-CA	53.3	9.4	Democrat
Sam Farr	17th District-CA	49.2	2.6	Democrat
Charlie Rangel	15th District-NY	47.9	30.5	Democrat
Maxine Waters	35th District-CA	47.4	34.1	Democrat
Harry Teague	2nd District-NM	47.3	1.6	Democrat
Devin Nunes	21st District-CA	43.4	2.1	Republican
Laura Richardson	37th District-CA	43.2	24.8	Democrat
Martin Heinrich	1st District-NM	42.6	2.3	Democrat
Dennis Cardoza	18th District-CA	41.9	5.6	Democrat
Lois Capps	22nd District-CA	41.7	1.9	Democrat

Source: National Journal's *Almanac of American Politics*, 2009.

TABLE 1.2. *Percentage Latino in Seven States and United States, 1950–2000 (Census Bureau)*

	1950	1960	1970	1980	1990	2000	2004
New Mexico	–	–	37	37	38	42	42
California	–	–	14	19	26	32	34
Texas	–	–	18	21	26	32	34
Arizona	–	–	17	16	19	25	25
Florida	–	–	7	9	12	17	18
New York	–	–	8	10	12	15	16
New Jersey	–	–	4	7	10	13	14
United States of America	1.5	2	5	6	9	13	14

In the fifty state legislatures, most Latino representatives have been elected from majority-Latino districts, but there are also some Latino legislators who have been elected from districts without Latino majorities. In 2004, 157 Latino legislators represent majority-Latino districts, including 132 Latino legislators from the seven states analyzed in this book (New Mexico, California, Texas, Arizona, Florida, New York, and New Jersey).[3] Sixty-five Latinos currently serve non-Latino majority districts.

[3] A rationale for these seven states will be discussed later in the book.

TABLE 1.3. *Percentage Latino in Seven State Legislatures and Congress,*
1986–2002

	1986	1990	1994	1998	2002	2004
New Mexico	30	34	38	35	39	40
California	6	5	10	15	22	24
Texas	13	15	19	20	19	20
Arizona	13	13	11	10	18	18
Florida	5	7	9	9	9	10
New York	3	3	5	6	6	7
New Jersey	1	1	1	3	4	5
US Congress	2	2	2	3	4	5

Source: Percentages computed based on National Directory of Latino Elected Officials
(published by the National Association of Latino Elected and Appointed Officials),
1986–present.

Table 1.3 shows the growth of Latinos serving in Congress and the
seven legislatures since 1986. The most pronounced growth since 1986
has been in California, where the percentage of Latinos serving in the
Legislature increased from 6 percent in 1986 to 24 percent in 2005. In all
seven states, the percentage of Latinos serving in legislatures has increased
substantially since 1986. In 1986, Latinos comprised 30 percent of the
New Mexico Legislature. Latinos now comprise 42 percent of the New
Mexico Legislature, slightly higher than the corresponding percentage of
Latinos in the state population. The reasons why New Mexico is so different are explored in Chapter 3. Some states, such as New York, have experienced growth in the percentage of Latinos serving in the Legislature, but
not nearly as significant as the growth in California or Texas. The reasons
for these differences are also explored in Chapter 3.

Literature on Latinos in Legislatures

The literature on Latino representation in the U.S. Congress is quite
sparse, although political scientists have conducted several studies in
recent years. The earliest work on Latino representation borrowed heavily
from previous work on African-American representation in Congress.
Table 1.4 lists some of the major works on race and representation since
1984, and most deal with African-American representation in the U.S.
Congress. This table describes the key research question of the work, the
dependent variable (s), and the methodology used. Note that statistical
analyses are by far the most utilized method, indicating the prevalence of

TABLE 1.4. *Literature on Racial and Ethnic Representation in U.S. State Legislatures*

Author (s)	Research Question	Dependent Variable(s)	Methodology
Welch & Hibbing (1984)	Do Latino members of Congress vote differently than non-Latino members?	Conservative coalition scores	Regression Analyses
Swain (1993)	Do black representatives better represent black constituents?	LCCR scores	Regression analyses and case studies
Hero & Tolbert (1995)	Are Latinos substantively represented?	Southwest Voter Research Initiative scores for 100th congress	Regression analyses
Kerr and Miller (1997)	Are Latinos substantively represented?	Southwest Voter Research Initiative scores for 100th congress	Regression analyses
Whitby (1997)	What is the link between black populations and House member behavior?	LCCR and other key votes	Regression analyses/ logistic and OLS
Lublin (1997)	Are majority-minority districts needed to elect minority legislators?	DW-NOMINATE scores; percent minority in district	Regression analyses/ logistic and OLS
Canon (1999)	Do black majority districts promote politics of difference?	Cosponsored bills, speeches, LCCR scores	Regression analyses, content analyses, case studies, interviews
Tate (1999)	Do blacks need to be descriptively represented in Congress to be well represented?	Votes on major legislation, NBES for black constituent attitudes	Regression analyses
Bratton (2006)	What is the effect of the Latino population on state legislative behavior?	Committee assignments, bill passage, and bill sponsorship	Regression analyses/negative binomial and logistic

roll call voting analyses. In the next several paragraphs, these works are discussed in more detail.

Many scholars assumed Latinos were a monolithic group, generally more liberal than whites were and much more similar in terms of political behavior to African Americans. Welch and Hibbing (1984) noted that Latino Conservative Coalition scores were more liberal than non-Latino representative scores. This study, however, only examined members from 1973 to 1980. It was not until 1992 that members of Mexican, Puerto Rican, and Cuban groups were simultaneously represented in Congress. Earlier Latino representatives were mostly Mexican Americans who are one of the more liberal Latino groups in the United States.

Hero and Tolbert (1995) went beyond Welch and Hibbing's (1984) earlier analysis by using Southwest Voter Research Initiative (SWVRI) scores for the 100th Congress to gauge the representation of Latinos and their interests. In their analysis, Hero and Tolbert found that high SWVRI scores for Latino representatives were not significantly different from non-Latino representatives.[4] In essence, they found that Latinos might benefit from "collective representation" and that dyadic representation was not evident. Kerr and Miller (1997) responded to this article by arguing that dyadic representation of Latino interests was in fact present. For them, "dyadic and collective representation can and do occur simultaneously in the political system and, as an analytical matter, should be considered together" (Kerr and Miller 1997, 1071). Although exposing some methodological problems with the paper, Kerr and Miller do not provide the necessary prescriptions for a better analysis. For example, the SWVRI scores in question are few in number and only cover the 100th Congress. Updated data reflecting the latest increases in the Latino population are needed for a more comprehensive analysis, as Chapter 6 will demonstrate.

David Lublin (1997) uses Poole-Rosenthal NOMINATE scores as the dependent variable for his analyses. Poole-Rosenthal scores do a much better job of assessing the political ideology of members of Congress because they include all votes, not just a few select votes, such as Americans for Democratic Action, American Conservative Union, or Southwest Voter Research Institute scores. The Poole-Rosenthal scores are continuously distributed, unlike interest group ratings, which are lumpy (Lublin 1997).

---

[4] SWVRI scores measure the extent to which legislators voted in support of a "Latino agenda" as determined by an umbrella group of Latino organizations. High scores indicate legislative voting records with support of Latino issues.

Lublin interacts the percentage of Latino population with the party of the representative and finds that Republican members are more conservative when they have higher Latino populations, whereas Democratic legislators are significantly more liberal (Canon 1999a; Lublin 1997b). Lublin explains this by noting that Democratic legislators tend to represent Mexican Americans and Puerto Ricans whereas Republican legislators generally represent Cuban Americans.

Another, more recent study examining Latino representation in Congress is Espino's (2003) work analyzing roll call voting data from the 103rd to 107th Congresses. He finds little support for the contention that members of the Congressional Hispanic Caucus vote more often with their fellow caucus members than they do with other members from their state delegations or with legislators who share their ideologies.

Another significant drawback of previous research on Latino representation is that it has focused almost exclusively on the U.S. Congress. Whereas this book does explore the election of Latinos to Congress, the value-added analyses will focus on the much-neglected state legislatures (regarding Latino representation). Additionally, previous research has focused heavily on the extent of Latino substantive representation without first answering some basic questions about descriptive representation. For example, Kathleen Bratton's (2006) recent study demonstrates that in seven U.S. legislatures, the presence of Latino legislators and Latino constituents has important implications for legislative behavior and success. Few scholars have inquired about what kind of districts tend to elect Latino legislators and analyzed how a district's ethnic composition affects the probability of electing Latino legislators (Grofman and Handley 2001; Lublin 1997). Moreover, few have asked how Latino legislators see themselves and the issues *they* care about in their districts. Chapter 5 will argue that Latino legislators see themselves in distinctive ways as demonstrated by a series of interview questions conducted with more than twenty legislators from diverse backgrounds and districts.

Other Minorities in Legislatures and Redistricting

The literature on African Americans and women in legislatures has provided unique insights into how minorities have been elected to Congress, which may be applicable to Latinos but not entirely appropriate. Most of the research regarding African Americans in legislatures has tended to focus on the U.S. Congress. In the area of racial representation, Carol Swain's (1993) *Black Faces, Black Interests* is an analysis of how

African Americans are represented in Congress. Swain's interviews with African-American members of Congress provide great insight into the varying styles within the African-American community. Her analyses of former Rep. Mike Espy (D-MS) and Rep. John Conyers (D-MI) show just how differently African-American members of Congress responded to their constituencies in order to secure re-election. In a similar way, Rep. Lincoln Díaz-Balart (R-FL) and Rep. Xavier Becerra (D-CA) represent their districts in different ways, which is more often the case with Latinos who have a much wider range of experiences. Swain's fundamental thesis that blacks would be better served by electing Democratic members of Congress, regardless of race, has been a controversial one. For example, Canon (1999a) notes that Swain does not account for all white representatives in districts with at least a 25-percent African-American population in the 103rd Congress. Because Latinos are not as solidly Democratic as African Americans, it does not follow that merely electing more Democrats to Congress would necessarily be a positive thing for the Latino community. On the contrary, political parties are increasingly courting Latino voters precisely because of their willingness to vote in less predictable ways.

In the case of Latinos, we have definitely seen more biracial coalitions but not always with African Americans (Casellas 2009b). In his book, *Race, Redistricting, and Representation*, David Canon (1999a) defends what he terms a "supply-side" theory of racial redistricting. He argues that the type of racial representation that exists in a district is dependent on the racial composition of contenders in the Democratic primary. In his view, the demand-side of the equation (voters) is less instrumental than the supply-side (candidates). Thus, at times, Latinos join forces with whites *against* the African-American community's favored candidate. Mayor Richard M. Daley (D-Chicago), for example, was initially elected with a Latino-white coalition. This coalition appears in many legislative districts in Democratic primaries.

Recent studies regarding African Americans and Latinos in legislatures indicate that the growing numbers of minorities in legislatures have resulted in the advancement of minority interests (Haynie 2001; Preuhs and Hero 2009). The debate regarding the value of descriptive representation for yielding substantive representation is an important one that has been debated by Mansbridge (1999), Canon (1999b), and Whitby (1997), who place a greater emphasis on descriptive representation, whereas Hero and Tolbert (1995) and Swain (1993) place a greater emphasis on substantive representation. Most studies on representation take for granted what we know about descriptive representation and leap to questions about substantive representation. This book fills the gap in the descriptive representation literature by arguing that simply assuming that demographic growth is the only way for increasing Latino representation misses the key institutional and state-level differences that help explain the election of Latino candidates. It also fills the gaps in the Latino representation literature by expanding our knowledge of the election of Latinos to state legislatures, with rich insights gained from the collection of large state- and district-level data, participant observation, and interviews with more than twenty Latino legislators from all parts of the country.

In addition, research previously done on African-American representation must be updated in light of the differences between both minority groups and the contributions of scholars of legislative politics. Previous studies on racial representation have not been as successful as they could be in synthesizing findings about race and ethnicity with the more general findings about legislative elections and legislative behavior.

Studies of women in legislatures have been plentiful, and we know that Latinas have different electoral strategies and outcomes in legislative races than Latinos. Copeland et al (2004) find that women legislators tend to come from more liberal, northern, and better educated states. Perhaps a more important finding in their study is that the supply of candidates is the one variable common to the success of both women and African Americans. Burrell (1990) makes the important point that the presence of women in legislative institutions has important agenda-setting implications. Fraga and Navarro (2004) have found that Latinas in Texas tend to identify more with women than with Latinas, whereas the opposite is true in California, yet at the same time, Latinas in general are more liberal than Latinos are and less likely to support increases in defense spending. In this sense, Latinas are no different from women writ large (Bratton and Haynie 1999). Latinas have also been more successful winning U.S. House races in California than in Texas. Additionally, states with multimember districts, like Arizona and New Jersey, tend to have higher percentages of Latinas serving in legislatures.

The literature on African Americans and Latinos in legislatures, however, is incomplete in that studies to date have not adequately addressed the conditions under which Latinos are elected to Congress and state legislatures in the first place. We know about how Latino members of Congress vote (Espino 2003; Lublin 1997), but not the conditions under which they are elected to their districts. Additionally, we know very little about the conditions under which Latinos are elected to state legislatures – the very bodies in which many Latino members of Congress previously served. Too much of the existing literature focuses on roll call voting in Congress, with insufficient attention devoted to how Latino legislators are elected to legislative bodies, how Latino legislators view themselves, and the effects of institutional structures and public policies such as term limits on Latino representation. Yet another limitation in the existing literature is that to date, no study compares Latino roll call voting in Congress with roll call voting in state legislatures.[5]

Research Questions

Some of the central questions driving this book are as follows: (1) Under what conditions are Latinos elected to Congress and to state legislatures? Although it is true that many Latinos are elected from majority-Latino districts, substantial numbers of Latino legislators do not represent districts with majority-Latino populations. (2) How much does the ethnic composition of a district affect the chances that a Latino candidate will get elected to office? Challengers to incumbents often face an uphill climb in their efforts to be elected to a given office. Latino candidates may find it advantageous to run in a district with a majority-minority population. However, only one Latino in the U.S. House represents a majority-white district. (3) How much does the ethnic composition of a district affect the chances that a Latino candidate will be elected in a given district? At least at the national level, very little evidence exists that Latinos are being elected from districts with white majorities. To date, only one district with a combined white and Latino population majority has elected a Latino member of Congress. At the state level, this pattern differs, which is why it is crucial to understand the variables that contribute to Latino victories at the state level.

I argue that Latinos are primarily elected from districts with substantial majorities of Latino citizens, much in the same pattern as African Americans. However, Latinos can be assisted by institutional characteristics, such as the type of legislature. The probability of electing Latinos to the legislature will vary by state, depending on a host of variables. Some of the explanatory variables that help explain the election of Latino

---

[5] We must, of course, be careful about direct comparisons between Congress and state legislatures, because the type of legislation and issues do vary within and across legislative bodies.

legislators are district demographics (percentage Latino in district and percentage African American in district) and the belief that Latinos will have more difficulty getting elected to the upper chamber. Latino candidates are more likely to run in districts with higher percentages of Latinos because their chances of winning would disproportionately increase (See Table 1.1 for Latino U.S. House representatives). I would expect these variables to have an impact on Latino descriptive representation in legislatures based on previous scholarship on Congressional elections.

Latinos are not unlike other candidates for legislative positions in the considerations that they employ to decide whether to run for office. Certainly, if an incumbent retires because of term limits and a seat becomes available, more candidates may decide to run for political office.[6] Incumbency no doubt confers enormous benefits, and challengers decide to run based on whether an incumbent is in the race. The ability to raise money matters too, but it is more critical for challengers than incumbents.[7] Incumbents decide to run in districts that will give them the highest probability of winning.

Representatives often come from districts with which they share similar demographic characteristics. Conversely, representatives choose to run in such districts. This is most clearly reflected in the way representatives interact with their constituents at home (Fenno 1978). Much in the same way Swain (1993) demonstrates that African Americans are more at ease with fellow African-American legislators, Latinos are also more likely to trust Latino representatives (Pantoja and Segura 2003). There is no question, then, that districts with higher proportions of Latinos will be more likely to support Latino candidates.

After explaining the conditions by which Latinos are elected to state legislatures and Congress, the key questions become: (1) What difference does it make whether Latinos are elected to Congress and state legislatures? By virtue of being Latino, legislators may care about different issues or more strongly advocate positions on a subset of issues, such as education policy. (2) To what extent do Latino legislators value descriptive representation? (3) More pointedly, do Latino legislators vote differently from others who represent similar constituencies? Studies of Latino public opinion have shown that Latinos tend to be fiscally liberal

---

[6] See Fowler and McClure (1990) for more on the dynamics of potential candidates in congressional districts, as well as the role of political ambition in determining who runs for Congress.

[7] See Cox and Katz (1996) and Jacobson (1997) for more on the incumbency advantage and factors determining who runs for congressional districts.

and socially conservative.[8] Many Latinos in Congress and state legislatures, however, appear to side with the Democratic Party on both fiscal and social issues. This section is an attempt to ascertain the extent to which Latinos differ from other representatives in terms of voting behavior. (4) Do Latino legislators emphasize different types of interests than other legislators who represent similar constituencies? Being Latino may explain why some legislators fight for causes not otherwise important to other groups. For example, Cuban American legislators may have a much more passionate view about the embargo on Cuba than other Latinos because of their personal experiences. Likewise, Mexican Americans will be more sensitive to immigration policy than Puerto Ricans because the policy more directly affects them and their immediate community.

Types of Data

I have collected comprehensive information on Latino elected officials in all seven of the state legislatures, as well as Congress. This will enable me to test the changes from 1990 to 2000 in terms of redistricting and the effect on Latino representation. The National Association of Latino Elected and Appointed Officials (NALEO) has identified Latino legislators for each chamber in the fifty states in an annual publication from 1984 to the present. The United States Census Bureau collected all the demographic data used in this study. The allocation of demographic data to legislative districts was done by each state and posted on state-maintained websites. The demographic variables are the percentage of a given district's population identified in the most recent census as Latino or African American. I have assembled additional demographic data for both current legislative districts and for districts before the 2001 redistricting cycle.

Using elite interviews and archival research, I have assembled the first-ever database of Latino legislators elected to non-Latino majority districts in all fifty states. As before, the identification of Latino legislators in each chamber was done by the NALEO. This section of the book, however, is not limited to the seven states. In fact, thirty-six of the sixty-five Latinos serving in non-Latino majority districts come from the other forty-three

---

[8] See Kaiser Foundation study for more details. The majority of Hispanics of all backgrounds (Cubans, Mexican Americans, and Puerto Ricans) believe in a larger role for government yet are opposed to abortion and gay rights legislation.

states. To determine whether a Latino represents a non-Latino majority district, I used Census Bureau data to determine the percentage of Latinos and African Americans in each district and compiled a database including this information. I also collected additional information on the district and the member, such as the political party of the member, the subethnic group of the member, the chamber of the member, whether the member was first elected in an open seat, the year first elected to any political office, and the year elected to the current office. This information was collected using Lexis-Nexis, candidate websites, state legislature websites, and phone calls to legislative staff members.

In the past several years, I have travelled to the annual meetings of the NALEO and the NHCSL. I have gleaned insights from participant observation in these meetings, which were heavily attended by Latino legislators from nearly all parts of the country. I also conducted in-depth interviews with more than twenty Latino legislators from diverse backgrounds (see Table 5.1 for descriptive statistics). The bulk of Chapter 5's data and analysis stem from these interviews and participant observation at these meetings.

I also use parts of the dataset assembled by David Lublin in his analysis of Congressional roll call voting. His dataset includes Poole-Rosenthal scores and additional demographic variables for U.S. House districts from the 87th through the 101st Congress.[9] I have added Poole-Rosenthal DW-NOMINATE scores from the 102nd Congress through the 104th Congress to Lublin's dataset.[10] Important variables to notice in this dataset include dummy variables for Cuban, Mexican, and Puerto Rican representatives.[11] This dataset is the most comprehensive available for studying Latino representation at the national level.

I also use a dataset assembled by Nolan McCarty for analysis of state legislative roll call voting. His dataset ascribes Poole-Rosenthal NOMINATE scores to members of most state legislatures in 1999 and 2001 for Colorado, New Jersey, and Texas. I have merged his dataset about roll call voting with my dataset about candidate ethnicity and district demographics to determine the impact of Latino districts and Latino legislators on legislative behavior.

---

[9] Data analyses conducted using STATA statistical software (Intercooled Stata 7.0).
[10] DW-NOMINATE scores are used in this analysis because such scores are comparable within and across Congresses.
[11] To date, all Latinos elected to the House of Representatives have been Cuban, Mexican, or Puerto Rican.

Choice of Legislatures

In addition to Congress, the seven state legislatures that are included in Chapter 3 of this study are New Mexico, California, Texas, Arizo`na, Florida, New York, and New Jersey. I chose these seven states and Congress because of their geographic and subethnic-group diversity in order to rule out region-specific or subethnic-group anomalies. These are the states with the largest percentage of Latinos, but states like Nevada have recently experienced a surging Latino population and could very well have been included in this study. Random selection of states does not work because some states have a tiny Latino population and no Latino legislators, thus making analysis impossible.

These states all have significant and growing Latino populations. New Mexico is an obvious choice because of its 42 percent Latino population and equally high percentage of Latinos in its legislature. California is the only majority-minority state. It has a 34 percent Latino population, and its legislature is one-quarter Latino. Like California, Texas has a 34 percent Latino population, but the percentage of Latinos in the Texas Legislature is 20 percent. Latinos comprise one-quarter of Arizona's population, and 18 percent of the Legislature is Latino. Florida's Latinos number 18 percent of the population, whereas 9 percent of the Legislature is Latino. In New York, Latinos comprise 16 percent of the population but only 6 percent of the Legislature. In New Jersey, Latinos comprise 14 percent of the state, whereas only 4 percent of the state legislators are Latino.[12]

The next chapter assesses the effects of turnover, term limits, and other institutional and demographic determinants of Latino representation in all state legislatures.

---

[12] Percentage Latino in state obtained from NALEO 2004 Election Handbook (see http://www.naleo.org), whereas percentage Latino in legislatures obtained from my own research (see Chapter 3).

2

The Effects of Population, Turnover, and Term Limits on Latino Representation

To what extent has the growing Latino population translated into more Latino legislators in Congress and state legislatures? Are Latinos as likely to serve in upper chambers as lower chambers? Are Latino candidates advantaged when turnover is high within legislatures? Does the imposition of term limits further advantage Latino candidates? Are states that are more liberal more likely than conservative states to elect Latino candidates? This chapter examines Latino representation in all fifty states by tracking the growth of Latinos serving in legislatures over the past decade and comparing the percentage of Latino citizens in the population with the percentage of Latinos in each legislature. At the *state* level, the Latino representation in the legislature is largely reflective of the percentage of Latinos in the population. Additionally, some states have much higher turnover rates in their legislatures, thus opening up more seats for talented Latinos to win. Similarly, Latinos may have better chances of being elected in states that have enacted term limits, which eliminates the incumbency advantage. Using the latest data on turnover and term limits, I help explain the impact of these variables on Latino representation in legislatures (Moncrief, Niemi, and Powell 2004). Chapter 3 explores the conditions under which Latinos are elected to seven of the nine state legislatures with the largest Latino memberships, and will provide precise estimates of *district-level* effects.

Latino Representation in State Lower and Upper Chambers
The pattern for most states is that Latino descriptive representation lags, due to many factors, including historically low rates of voter turnout,

a large number of undocumented immigrants, and higher rates of non-citizenship among Latinos. At the same time, we find some variation between lower and upper chambers across the state legislatures. As Figures 2.1 and 2.2 show, by 2000, New Mexico remained an outlier, but California had shown a dramatic increase in Latino representation compared to 1992. Florida's Latino population has increased in eight years, but Latino legislative representation in the lower chamber has remained stagnant. Nevada's Latino population has also substantially increased, yet Latino legislative representation has not risen with this phenomenon. The pattern for upper chambers looks very similar to lower chambers, with the exception of a few states, such as Florida and Nevada, which have a much higher percentage of Latinos in the State Senate than in the House. As in the lower chamber, the percentage of Latinos serving in the California Senate increased over the eight-year period. Only in Arizona and Texas did the percentage of Latinos serving in the Senate increase vis-à-vis 1992. In Florida, the Latino population increased from about 12 percent to 17 percent, yet the percentage of Latinos in the State Senate decreased to less than 10 percent of the total. By 2004, we have seen only minor changes from 2000. Colorado had a slight decrease in Latino representation in the House, whereas the Senate exhibited little change (most probably because of the longer terms).

Turnover, Professionalization, and Term Limits

I expect that states with higher percentages of Latinos in the population would have higher percentages of Latinos in the legislature.[1] The percentage of Latinos in both upper and lower chambers is substantially below the corresponding percentage of Latinos in the state population. New Mexico is clearly an outlier in that there is parity between the state population and legislative descriptive representation. Arizona and Texas are the only other states with double-digit representation in their legislatures, despite the fact that six other states had more than a 10 percent Latino population in 1992.

Few studies have examined the effect of the Latino population, legislative professionalization, and state legislative term limits on Latino representation. As Moncrief et al. (1996) observe, "[w]hile there has

---

[1] Just as districts with higher proportions of Latinos will be more likely to elect Latino candidates, as the Latino population increases in a state, the percentage of Latinos in the legislature should also increase (Lublin 1997).

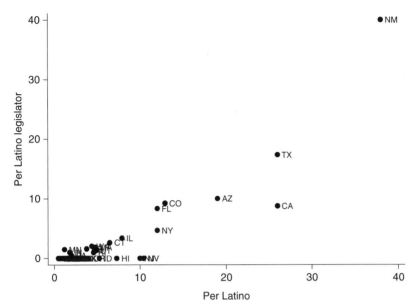

FIGURE 2.1. Latino representation in state lower houses, 1992.

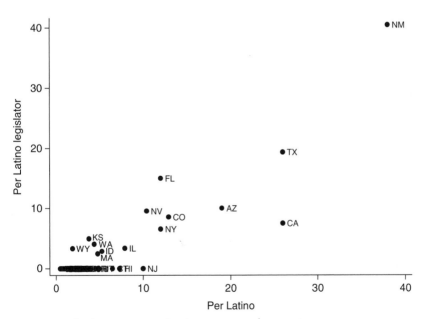

FIGURE 2.2. Latino representation in state upper houses, 1992.

TABLE 2.1. *Term Limits Legislation in the United States*

State	Year Enacted	Impact Year
Arizona	1992	2000
Arkansas	1992	1998 House
		2000 Senate
California	1990	1996 House
		1998 Senate
Colorado	1990	1998
Florida	1992	2000
Louisiana	1995	2007
Maine	1993	1996
Michigan	1992	1998 House
		2002 Senate
Missouri	1992	2002
Montana	1992	2000
Nebraska	2000	2006
Nevada	1996	2010
Ohio	1992	2000
Oklahoma	1990	2004
S. Dakota	1992	2000

Source: National Council of State Legislatures. Excluded are states that passed term limits that were either overturned by the courts or repealed by the legislature.

been research on the consequences of women in state legislatures, similar research on the effect of African-American or Hispanic legislators has been lacking" (310). Broader studies have tended to focus on the impact of term limits on turnover, membership composition, legislative professionalization, and partisanship (Fiorina 1994, 1999; Meinke and Hasecke 2003; Moncrief, Niemi, and Powell 2004). Because many states adopted term limits in the early 1990s, the long-term effects of this policy are only beginning to emerge (see Table 2.1).

The literature on women in legislatures has largely focused on the effects of having women in legislatures (Kathlene 1994; Richardson and Freeman 1995; Thomas and Welch 1991). Some studies have examined the effect of reapportionment and the electability of women to legislative institutions, although not explicitly the effect of term limits (Bullock 1992; Grofman and Handley 1989; Nelson 1991; Philpot and Walton 2007).

But are Latinos really newcomers to the political system? In most states, this is true, but in states like New Mexico, Latinos have long been a part of the political process at the elite level (Vigil 1996). In New York and California, the growth of the Latino population has been quite stark in the last decade. This trend is likely to grow, and we are beginning to see the growth of Latino elected officials in unlikely areas of the country, and with the support of white voters rather than just coethnics. As Moncrief et al. (2000) argue, the number of minority legislators would undoubtedly grow if political parties and interest groups made concerted efforts to recruit and fund potential candidates. Fowler (1992) has observed (in the context of women legislators) that the basic problem is that too few women run in most states, either in primaries or in general elections, to produce measurable increases in female representation. This has arguably been the case with Latinos, despite their growing electoral influence.

State-Level Diversity

Why might higher proportions of Latinos in a state be related to higher proportions of Latino legislators? As Hero and Tolbert (1996) have argued, a state's racial and ethnic diversity can have important implications for minority groups, especially in homogenous states. The Latino populations in the states are also characterized by differences based on national origin and political incorporation in state politics. Increased diversity at the state level can also create an environment more conducive to the election of minorities. Additionally, such diversity can also have an impact on the election of Latinos to districts that are not ethnically diverse because of the state-level diversity. As Gay (2001) argues, minorities are more likely to trust members of their own group. In addition, Pantoja and Segura (2003) show that as the number of Latinos serving in the legislature increases, levels of political alienation among Latino voters decrease, arguably because of the trust Latinos place in members of their own ethnicity to help solve the problems affecting their community. Barreto, Segura, and Woods (2004) show that Latinos are more likely to turn out when they live in majority-Latino districts. As Bobo and Gilliam (1990) have demonstrated as the "empowerment" hypothesis, minorities become more likely to participate and vote in politics as their numbers in elected positions increase. In particular, when Latinos are represented in large numbers in a state legislature, even white voters become more willing to support Latinos for elective offices. For instance, Bill Richardson (D-NM) was elected governor in a state with a large Latino population (43 percent) precisely because of his ability to appeal to both Latinos and whites in the state.

Hence, the first hypothesis is:

Demography Hypothesis: *The percentage of Latinos in a state's population will be positively associated with the representation of Latinos in the legislature.*

High Rates of Turnover Help Newcomers to the Political Process

In recent years, legislative scholars have been interested in explaining the rates of turnover across the states. Turnover rates had declined throughout the 1980s, but the advent of term limits in many states in the 1990s seemed likely to increase turnover rates once again (Niemi and Winsky 1987). Fifteen states currently have term limits. Most term limits legislation was passed in the early 1990s, although there are several key exceptions. Other states, such as Idaho and Oregon, had passed term limits legislation, but the courts or the state legislature proceeded to invalidate them. Of the fifteen states, only a few are states with relatively high percentages of Latinos. Arizona, California, Colorado, and Florida all have significant Latino populations, whereas the other eleven states are generally more conservative with few minorities. According to Breaux and Jewell (1992), the lower turnover rates in the 1980s were due to lower rates of voluntary retirements. It makes sense that states with legislative term limits would see higher levels of turnover and interchamber movement. Indeed, whether a state has a professional legislature, and when term limits were adopted and implemented, all have effects on the turnover percentage (Moncrief, Niemi, and Powell 2004).

Although most of the arguments for term limits revolve around getting rid of entrenched incumbents, there is a possibility that this policy has actually helped minorities by opening up seats that would have otherwise not been available to political newcomers. Because Latinos are political newcomers, the effect of term limits and turnover on Latino representation demands scholarly attention. I would expect that states with term limits would have a positive association with the percentage of Latinos in legislatures. That is, legislative term limits may actually increase the ability of Latinos to win in state legislative races. Moreover, related to term limits, I would expect that states with higher percentages of legislative turnover would more likely be associated with higher levels of Latino representation for many of the same reasons. As political neophytes compared to African Americans, Latinos stand to benefit from open seats, especially in states that have seen exponential rates of growth among the Latino community.

The little work on the effects of term limits on the representation of minorities and women demonstrate some positive findings for Latino

candidates. Carroll and Jenkins (2001) find that more women were turned
out of office by term limits in 1998 and 2000 than were elected to seats
open because of term-limited incumbents. They also find that the number
of minorities in term-limited state lower chamber seats increased following the elections of 1998 and 2000. Even though they are not specifically
concerned with Latinos in their analysis, they stipulate their findings are
"somewhat more promising for Latinos who were able to win several
term-limited seats in districts where Latinos were a minority (and even a
small minority). The findings suggest that Latinos may continue to benefit
from term limits if strong Latino candidates who can appeal to primarily
white constituencies continue to come forward" (Carroll and Jenkins
2001, 12). As Canon (1999) notes, "states continue to serve as laboratories of experimentation... state-level variation [regarding]...term limits
allows some additional leverage on representational questions; research
on these topics should help inform debates at the national level" (371). In
line with Canon's call for more research, this chapter seeks to explain the
effects of term limits and legislative turnover on Latino representation
in the fifty states. That is, term limits may have an unintended positive
effect on Latino representation by replacing entrenched incumbents with
newcomers to the political system.

Work by political scientists in the late 1990s involved the development of models based on past turnover rates and the length of term limits (Francis and Kenney 1997). In 2000, Francis and Kenney proposed
a theory of "churning" by which members would leave legislatures for
other careers in anticipation of the turnover deadline. These theories no
doubt apply to all legislators regardless of race, ethnicity, or gender, but
this study seeks to test whether Latinos have been particularly helped or
hurt by such policies. Accordingly,

Turnover Hypothesis: *State legislatures with higher turnover rates will have a*
higher representation of Latinos in the legislature.

State legislatures are not one-size-fits-all institutions. Scholars have dis-
tinguished the level of professionalization of legislatures based on how
often they meet, how much legislators are paid, and the size of the staff
(Fiorina 1994; Hero 1992). Some state legislatures, like New York's,
are highly professional. That is, legislators are paid a comfortable salary (about $80,000 per year), meet quite often, and have other benefits.
Other legislatures, like New Mexico, are known as citizen legislatures.
They often do not receive a salary, meet a couple of months during the

year, and consequently have higher rates of turnover.[2] Fiorina (1994) has hypothesized that professional legislatures are more conducive to the election of Democrats, since potential Democratic candidates tend to come from the public sector and would be attracted by a comfortable position. Although it is true that most Latinos are Democrats, we cannot deduce that Latinos will fare better in professional legislatures for several reasons. First, Latinos are political newcomers, unlike African Americans or labor union candidates. Political newcomers, by definition, have not amassed the networks and name recognition needed to win highly desirable seats. Second, any position that is highly desirable is bound to attract more applicants. Just as we do not see too many Latino CEOs, it is also unlikely for Latinos to be able to compete as successfully for such desirable positions.

Institutional Design Matters

If we assume that candidates are rational actors who balance the costs and benefits of seeking elective office, we can conclude that more individuals would be attracted to higher-paying legislatures than low-paying legislatures (Mayhew 1974; Downs 1957; Arnold 1990). A perfect example of a professional legislature is New York, which provides a generous compensation of $79,500 per year for members of the legislature, in addition to a "lulu" aimed at covering expenses.[3] Because citizen legislatures are less desirable, the pool of candidates should be smaller, which should benefit political newcomers. Latinos are political newcomers, so I would suspect, then, that states with citizen legislatures would more likely be associated with greater levels of Latino representation because turnover is higher and competition is less fierce for these seats, giving disadvantaged groups better opportunities to win.[4] This leads to the third hypothesis:

Institutional Design Hypothesis: *States with professional legislatures will have lower representation of Latinos in the legislature.*

---

[2] In New Mexico, legislators received a salary of $8,460 in 2005, according to the Council of State Governments.

[3] This makes New York a "professional" legislature, unlike many other states that have a "citizen" legislature that pays minimal salaries and meets less often.

[4] In nearly every state, the Latino population has substantially grown in the past twenty years. Term limits were not enacted until the mid 1990s in most states. During the time associated with this study, the number of Latinos serving in legislatures has increased, although not to the extent the population has. That Latinos are political newcomers vis-à-vis other groups such as African-Americans is indisputable.

Methods

I test these hypotheses by analyzing data in presidential election years from 1992 to 2004. No states had passed legislative term limits prior to 1990. Data regarding the percentage of Latino citizens in each state is from the United States Census Bureau[5]. I computed the percentage of Latinos serving in each legislature by consulting the National Directory of Latino Elected Officials published annually. Moncrief, Niemi, and Powell generously provide data involving term limits and turnover based on their article published in August 2004. Data measuring the extent of professionalization come from Squire (2007).[6] I obtained data on citizen ideology first developed by Erickson, Wright, and McIver (1993) and later refined by Wright (2004). Because of Nebraska's unicameral legislature, I code it as an upper chamber. I conduct the analysis for the two chambers combined with a dummy variable for the chamber. I analyze each legislature beginning with the 1992 presidential election, every four years until 2004.

Variables

The dependent variable is the percentage of Latinos serving in each chamber in each state legislature. I have identified Latino legislators in each chamber by consulting the National Association of Latino Elected and Appointed Officials (NALEO).[7] The United States Census Bureau collected the demographic data. The demographic variables are the percentage of a given state's population who are identified in the most recent census as Latino citizens.

---

[5] The percentage of Latino citizens in a state as collected by the Census Bureau is the most accurate measure available comparing the Latino population. The percentage of Latino voters in a state is not included in this analysis for a couple of reasons. First, I am interested in the connection between the Latino population of a state and the influence of Latinos in state legislatures. Second, just because some Latinos are not registered to vote, do not vote, or are not eligible to vote does not mean that they cannot, do not, and/or should not have influence in the political process. Members of Congress have been shown to be particularly sensitive to the potential preferences of people in their districts (Arnold 1990). Politicians are therefore quite aware that many Latinos will register and eventually vote, thus changing the demographics of districts all across the country.

[6] There is no significant correlation between professionalization and percentage Latino in a state. Whereas California has a professional legislature, Florida, New Mexico, and Texas have citizen legislatures. That is, highly professional legislatures are not always in medium to large states.

[7] I have confirmed NALEO's listing of Latino legislators by comparing their list with the National Hispanic Caucus of State Legislators (NHCSL) roster.

The explanatory variables also include the percentage of Latino citizens in the population for all fifty states and the entire nation. I use U.S. Census data collected from the American Community Survey to estimate the percentage of Latino citizens in the district, as well as estimates from the William Velazquez Institute (see http://www.wcvi.org). A dummy variable is included for the upper chamber (1 if upper chamber; 0 otherwise).

Two dummy variables are also included for states with term limits. The first term limit variable measures the year term limits were enacted. For example, if term limits were enacted in 1992 for a particular state, this observation is coded for that year and any year afterward until implementation. The rationale here is that the enactment of term limits may have an anticipatory effect on legislators, who may decide to alter their career plans based on future limits. The second term limit variable measures the year term limits took effect. This variable measures directly the effect of term limits on those legislators who are forced out of office by term limits. For example, if term limits became effective in a given state in 2000, then that observation is coded 1 for 2000 and 2004. For states that had term limits enacted or carried out in off years, such as 1995, then the observation is coded 1 for the subsequent year. States that initially passed term limits for legislators but were subsequently repealed either by the courts or by the legislature are coded 0. These states include Oregon, Idaho, and Utah. In addition, I track the percentage turnover in the lower and upper chambers for all fifty states and Congress every four years along presidential election years.

I perform a feasible generalized least squares (FGLS) time-series regression in order to estimate the effects of the explanatory variables on the percentage of Latinos in legislatures over the time period from 1992 through 2004, every four years on the presidential election cycle. Because the repeated observations in the dataset are not independent, an FGLS model instead of an Ordinary Least Squares (OLS) model is necessary to avoid biased estimates. In particular, I use FGLS to address the problem of serial correlation evident in this dataset as it is in most time-series data (Worrall and Pratt 2004). That is, the percentage of Latinos serving in the legislature in 1992 is correlated with the percentage of Latinos serving in legislatures in 1996, 2000, and 2004. The Parks method is not used because of the many problems associated with the overconfidence of standard error estimates (Beck and Katz 1995).[8] For the sake

---

[8] The Parks method is feasible generalized least squares with the elimination of serial correlation of errors by examining the residuals to estimate "unit-specific serial correlation

of robustness, these models are also estimated using random and fixed effects generalized least squares (FGLS), as well as OLS, and for the most part the substantive results remain the same (more on this later). The percentage Latino in the population is based on the 1990 Census for 1992 and 1996, whereas the updated Census 2000 numbers are used for 2000 and 2004.

Institutional and Demographic Determinants of Latino Representation

As shown in Table 2.2, [T]here is a strong relationship between the percentage of Latino citizens in a state and the percentage of Latinos in the legislature. A bivariate model provides strong support for the demographic hypothesis.[9] It is still undoubtedly the case that Latino legislators are elected from states that have higher percentages of Latino citizens and even more so from districts that are majority-Latino. The overall percentage of Latinos in a state is also strongly related to the percentage of Latinos in the state legislature, although the relationship is not as strong.[10] This chapter also explores the conditions under which Latinos are elected to seven of the nine state legislatures with the largest Latino memberships, and the next chapter will provide precise estimates of district-level effects.

A multivariate regression including the two dummy variables for the enactment and implementation of term limits legislation is performed for 1992, 1996, 2000, and 2004.[11] The percentage of Latino citizens in a state remains a significant predictor. There is no evidence to suggest that Latino representation is affected in any way by the enactment of term limits legislation. The percentage turnover has positive but insignificant effects on Latino representation. As the percentage of new legislators rises in a state, the percentage of Latinos in a legislature also rises. Some older legislators may have retired, but it is difficult to conclude, based on the term limit dummy variable, that term limits in general have had a positive effect on Latino representation. It is the case, however, that the opening up of otherwise entrenched seats has a positive effect on Latino

of the errors, which are then used to transform the model into one with serially independent errors." See Beck and Katz (1995) for more on the different approaches to TSCS estimations.

[9] Appendix A shows the results of several other model specifications.

[10] This is based on a separate bivariate analysis not shown in Table 2.2 but available upon request.

[11] The N is 368, and not 396, because of some missing percentage turnover data in Moncrief et al's dataset.

TABLE 2.2. *The Effects of Turnover and Term Limits on Latino Representation, 1992, 1996, 2000, and 2004*

	Variables
Percentage Latino Citizens in State	.965***
	(.048)
Enactment of Term Limits	.071
	(.367)
Implementation of Term Limits	-1.09*
	(.512)
Percentage Turnover	.017
	(.009)
Chamber	-.115
	(.280)
State Ideology	.013**
	(.005)
Professionalization	1.59
	(2.16)
Professionalization X Percentage Latino Citizens in State	-.563**
	(.199)
Term Limits Imp X	.348***
Percentage Latino Citizens in State	(.057)
	(1.78)
Size of Legislature	.001
	(.003)
Constant	-2.45***
	(.669)
N	368
Years Included	1992
	1996
	2000
	2004

Notes: Entries are regression coefficients; standard errors in parentheses.
Feasible Generalized Least Squares Cross-Sectional Time-Series Regression.
*$p<.05$; **$p<.01$, ***$p<.001$

representation. In order to control for possible effects of the lower versus upper chamber, a dummy variable is included, which, as it turns out, is not associated with the percentage of Latinos serving in legislatures. There are no significant effects between the upper and lower chambers.

Additionally, whether a legislature is citizen or professional is an important variable to consider. I test whether a measure of professionalization first devised by Squire (2007) has significant effects on Latino representation. On its own, this measure is not significantly related to the percentage of Latino legislators. The implementation of term limits variable alone, however, has a negative effect on Latino representation. Why does the implementation of term limits have a negative effect on Latino representation, given that the direct result of these policies is to increase legislative turnover? This is because the implementation of term limits did not take place in states with significant Latino populations until after 2000 (only California and Colorado had term limit implementations before 2000).

Does the state's ideology have any effect on Latino representation? This variable is measured by the Wright (2004) citizen ideology data in the respective election year. As the model shows, the coefficient is in the hypothesized direction, as more liberal citizenries are more likely to elect Latino legislators.

Might professionalization and term limits be predictive of higher levels of Latino representation in states with higher proportions of Latino citizens? To test this, I interacted the Squire professionalism variable with the percentage of Latino citizens in the state to determine whether the key mechanism of predicting Latino representation in state legislatures is not merely the professionalization of the legislature, but whether this measure works in tandem with higher proportions of Latino citizens in the state. Indeed, this interaction has a significant effect on the presence of Latinos in legislatures. States with higher proportions of Latino citizens and less professional legislatures are significantly associated with higher proportions of Latino legislators. The enactment variable, although still statistically insignificant, sharply changes into the hypothesized direction, whereas the implementation variable remains a statistically significant predictor of Latino representation in legislatures. Between 2000 and 2004, the states of Arizona, Florida, Missouri, Montana, Ohio, Oklahoma, and South Dakota felt the impact of term limits legislation. Only Arizona and Florida have significant Latino populations in the legislature and the population, which helps explain the change in the implementation variable. Nevertheless, this finding suggests that the long-term effects of term limits may be changing with the demographic adjustments across the United States. That is Latinos are in fact just beginning to benefit from such policies. Moreover, it remains the case that legislatures that are more professional are less likely to be favorable to greater degrees of Latino representation, regardless of percentage turnover.

It is not professionalization per se that influences Latino representation, but the interactive effect of professionalization and the percentage of Latino citizens in the population that help explain Latino descriptive representation. Moreover, term limits are an important predictor of greater degrees of Latino representation, but the effect is particularly strong when the percentage of Latino citizens in a state and term limits combine to create the proverbial "perfect storm" of significantly higher degrees of Latino representation. Legislatures that are more professional are less likely to be favorable to greater degrees of Latino representation, even when controlling for percentage turnover.

Conclusion

Across five different model specifications, the percentage of Latinos in a state remained a strong positive effect on Latino descriptive representation in legislatures. Perhaps the most surprising finding is the negative effect of the implementation of term limits on Latino descriptive representation in legislatures. Based on rather intuitive reasons, I expected states with term limits to be positively associated with Latino legislative representation because of the idea that term limits led to higher turnover, and hence more opportunities for Latinos to get elected. It turns out that term limits and professionalization only have significant effects on Latino descriptive representation when interacted with the percentage of Latino citizens in a state. The implementation of term limits variable is significant with a negative coefficient on its own, but when interacted with the percent Latino citizen variable, it has a positive coefficient, suggesting that it is still too early to dismiss the idea that term limits have been a net negative or positive in terms of Latino representation.

Term limits working in tandem with increases in the percentage of Latino citizens in a state contribute to greater degrees of Latino representation. No support was discovered for the churning effect (i.e., enactment of term limits legislation leading legislators to prematurely retire). Of course, this may be true in general, but not for Latino legislators. The level of professionalization of the legislature does make a difference for Latino representation. The less professional a legislature is, the more likely it is to be associated with greater degrees of Latino representation, but only when interacted with the percentage of Latino citizens in the population. The interaction between the percentage of Latino citizens and the implementation of term limits helps explain Latino representation in the full model.

In the final analysis, these models suggest that higher percentages of Latinos in a state, more liberal citizenries, and the presence of citizen legislatures all positively contribute to Latino representation. States with low percentages of Latinos and professional legislatures are not good environments for the election of Latino candidates. Even though these analyses do not imply that term limits have been a good policy for Latino representation, they do show that citizen legislatures are better than professional legislatures for Latino candidates. This is undoubtedly because citizen legislatures offer low pay, less prestige, and less competition. These characteristics, in turn, lead to more opportunities for Latino candidates. This is why the New Mexico and Florida legislatures are conducive to the election of Latino candidates (see Chapter 3). In contrast, New York's highly professional legislature has been a difficult barrier for Latinos to cross. These findings have larger implications: Latinos and probably other minorities like African Americans are occupying legislative seats that are undesirable for whites, much in the same way Latinos and African Americans still do not occupy the most prestigious positions in the corporate world.[12] The less prestigious citizen legislatures provide more opportunities for Latinos than professional legislatures.

In what types of districts are Latinos winning? Carroll and Jenkins (2001) show that of the six Latinos in 1998 and the six Latinos in 2000 who won in seats affected by term-limited retirements, eight were elected in districts with predominantly white populations. In addition, one Latino in 1998 was elected in a 20 percent Latino district, whereas three Latinos in 1998 and four in 2000 were elected in districts with fewer than 12 percent Latino population. Chapter 4 will provide more in-depth analysis of the election of Latino candidates to non-Latino majority districts, but the evidence so far suggests that institutional determinants may have a positive impact on Latino representation.

Chapter 3 will delve deeper into the election of Latino candidates to legislatures by examining the conditions under which Latinos are elected to seven state legislatures. Focus will be on seven of the nine states with the highest Latino populations to determine whether certain states are more conducive to the election of Latino candidates. The analysis will provide probabilities of Latinos getting elected to certain districts given

---

[12] Thanks to Tali Mendelberg for pointing out this connection.

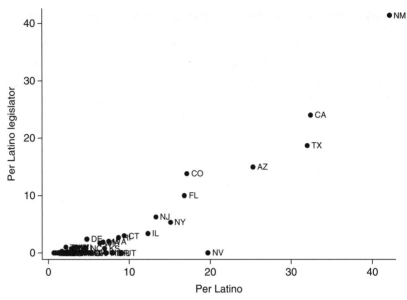

FIGURE 2.3. Latino representation in state lower houses, 2000.

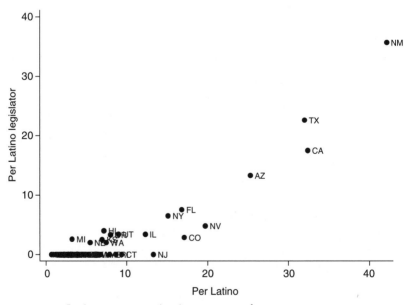

FIGURE 2.4. Latino representation in state upper houses, 2000.

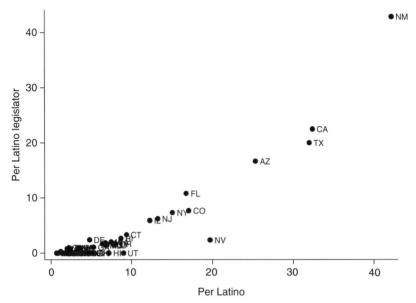

FIGURE 2.5. Latino representation in state lower houses, 2004.

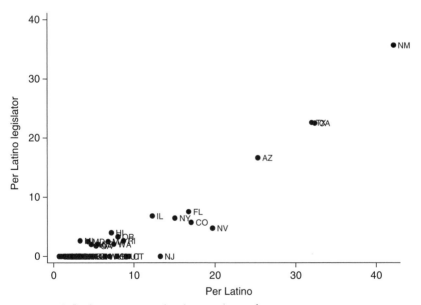

FIGURE 2.6. Latino representation in state upper houses, 2004.

the percentage of Latinos living in the district. In this sense, a more in-depth analysis of state-level institutional variation may provide for a more complete understanding of the dynamics affecting the election of Latino legislators. Specifically, the presence of multimember district schemes in states like Arizona and New Jersey have been shown to be a barrier to Latino representation (Gerber et al. 1998).

3

District Composition and the Election of Latino Candidates

"There is no elevator to the top. You have to take the stairs, and take it one step at time." – Dr. Juan Andrade on Latino electoral prospects

After having addressed the institutional and demographic determinants of Latino representation across all fifty states, this chapter delves into district-level determinants of Latino representation in states with significant Latino populations to estimate the probability of electing Latino candidates. In particular, this chapter addresses the following questions: How does the ethnic composition of a legislative *district* affect the probability that the district will elect a Latino candidate? Are Latino candidates advantaged when they run in districts with citizens who share their ethnic heritage? At what point does the ethnic composition of a district create an advantage for Latino candidates? Do districts need to be majority-Latino before they tend to elect Latino candidates, or is there a lesser threshold where Latino candidates become competitive? If so, what is that threshold? What about other minority groups? Does it matter how many African-American citizens reside in a district? Are Latino candidates advantaged when a district's African-American and Latino citizens outnumber a district's Anglo citizens?

Why might the ethnic composition of a district affect the chances of electing a Latino legislator? First, a district's composition affects the supply of candidates for potential office. In many instances, Latinos who have been successful in winning state legislative seats began their careers on school boards or city councils in heavily Latino districts. They first become well known in the local community. Later, they decide to run for state legislative seats when a seat becomes vacant or when the incumbent looks vulnerable. In U.S. House races, Jacobson (1997) argues that the party with the best opportunity to win runs the most experienced candidates. Canon (1990), however, finds that in elections in which one party dominates, amateurs run because experienced politicians in the winning party are unavailable or are unaware of the opportunity. Moreover, Grofman et al. (2001) argue that along with Republican dominance in Southern States after the Civil Rights Movement, it became easier for African Americans to win Democratic primaries, given the changing composition of the Democratic Party in that region. Berkman (1994) finds that in the case of state legislative races, *institutional context* must be taken into account because state legislators and school board members may weigh different considerations when deciding to run for office. Latinos are no different from other groups when deciding to run for office. They must assess the partisan nature of the district, the racial and ethnic makeup, the availability of financial resources, and the vulnerability of the incumbent when deciding to run (Fowler and McClure 1990; Jacobson and Kernell 1981; Kazee 1994; Maisel and Stone 1997).

This chapter provides evidence for the most basic of the central arguments of the book, that demographics is destiny. The percentage of Latino citizens in a district has an important and significant effect on the election of Latino legislatures. This has to do with not only the growing Latino population, but also the important elite-driven method of redistricting, especially following the 1990 Census.

Redistricting after the Voting Rights Act of 1965

The Voting Rights Act (VRA) has had profound effects on the composition of legislatures and Congress since its passage in 1965. Passed in order to remedy the discrimination African Americans faced at the polls in most Southern states, the VRA fundamentally changed the procedures states used when drawing new legislative districts following the decennial census. In particular, Section 5 has influenced how state legislatures have drawn district lines, especially since 1990. Section 5 provides that any changes to voting procedures or district boundaries must be "precleared" by the Department of Justice or the federal Appeals Court for the District of Columbia. Normally, the Department of Justice has used the preclearance procedure to ensure that no dilution or retrogression of minority voting rights would ensue from the new districts.

The 1980s and 1990s brought litigation regarding how to interpret the VRA with respect to the impact on minority communities. Following the reauthorization of the act in 1982, it became unclear precisely who could sue if districts were drawn in a discriminatory manner. The Court settled this issue in *Thornburg v. Gingles* (1986), with a three-pronged test making it more difficult for minority groups to claim discrimination under section 2. Later in the 1990s, the *Shaw* cases were notorious for their impact on racial gerrymandering. For example, the 12th district of North Carolina was ruled unconstitutional because it spanned the entire state along an interstate highway in order to create a majority-black district. In short, the court ruled that the creation of districts using race as a sole criterion was unconstitutional.[1] However, following the 1990 Census, several new Latino majority congressional districts were created facilitating the election of Latino members of Congress. Some critics of the creation of majority-minority districts have argued that descriptive representation undoubtedly increased but at a cost to substantive representation (Swain 1993) Four years later, Republicans took control of Congress, and several new minority members saw their influence in a majoritarian institution lessen overnight.

Although race-based redistricting has not disappeared, the Court has issued several guidelines for redistricting commissions and state legislatures. Traditional rules of redistricting require: (1) respect for political subdivisions and boundaries, (2) compactness, and (3) contiguity. As per the *Shaw* cases, bizarrely shaped districts created with race or ethnicity as the sole criterion and ignoring the above rules would not withstand judicial scrutiny. Another important consideration state legislatures use is protection of incumbents. Many had argued that they were not using race as a criterion but instead were trying to protect black incumbents. This argument was also rejected by the court.[2]

In the post-2000 era, perhaps the most significant court case dealing with redistricting was *Georgia v. Ashcroft*. This case had to do with Georgia's Democratic legislature creating a set of districts that spread black voters around instead of concentrating them in supermajority black districts. Governor Sonny Perdue, a Republican, sued, claiming that the VRA had violated the electoral opportunities of black voters. In a narrow decision, the Court ruled that the VRA was not violated because of this plan, largely because of the retrogression principle; that is, black voters' interests were ultimately helped by the districting scheme. In particular, Justice O'Connor relied on social scientific evidence to argue that

---

[1] *Miller v. Johnson* (1995).
[2] *Bush. v. Vera* (1996).

"coalitional districts" could in fact be better for the representation of minority interests (Bedoya 2006).

In a *Yale Law Journal* article critical of the court's decision, Bedoya (2006) notes that "coalitional districts in the Hispanic context ... may be insufficient to provide Hispanic voters an opportunity to elect their candidates of choice" (2125). In particular, Bedoya (2005) and Cartagena (2004) argue that Latinos may in fact be ill-served by the jurisprudential precedent set forth by Justice O'Connor in *Georgia v. Ashcroft*. In Congress, nearly all of the representatives come from such districts, but in state legislatures, Latinos have been elected in coalitional districts. Nevertheless, after this monumental case, the court adopts what it calls a "totality of circumstances" approach when determining the constitutionality of districts. That is, the court looks beyond descriptive representation to assess the degree to which that racial or ethnic group has achieved leadership and power in politics (Cartagena 2005).

The Department of Justice and the courts heavily regulate the creation of legislative districts at the state and federal level. No longer can race be used as the sole criterion in drawing legislative districts. This has made legislatures a bit more creative in how they draw districts, but at the same time, because of residential segregation, it is not unconstitutional to draw black or Latino majority districts if they are compact, contiguous, and respect traditional political boundaries. The next section turns to the extent of coethnic voting in legislative districts.

Ethnic and Racial Voting in Legislative Districts

Should we expect differences among the states, and if so, why? Some states, like Florida and New Mexico, should have higher probabilities of electing Latinos for many reasons. In Florida, it is well documented that Cuban Americans vote at higher rates than other Latino groups, so we should expect that Florida should be fairly conducive, whereas New York's largely Puerto Rican population votes in much lower numbers, so it should be more difficult for Latinos to win state legislative seats. This is despite the fact that Puerto Ricans do not have the obstacle of obtaining citizenship. Moreover, New York provides generous compensation to its legislatures. Because of its generous rate of pay, reasonable workload, no term limits, and redistricting agreements, New York has experienced little turnover in the Legislature in recent years (Ngai 2006). This has made it more difficult for Latinos to enter the political pipeline and win in districts that have entrenched white or African-American incumbents.

Whereas Latinos have been winning in districts with non-Latino majorities throughout the country, I will show that New York has not had much success in this regard, largely because of its professional legislature.

Coalitions between African Americans and Latinos have historically occurred in urban contexts. For example, in Los Angeles, New York, and Houston, Latinos have often joined with African Americans to elect preferred candidates (Kaufmann 2004). At times, Latinos join forces with whites *against* the African-American community's favored candidate (Vaca 2004). The election of Mayor Richard M. Daley (D-Chicago) is a case where his election was due in large part to a Latino-white coalition formed against African Americans. More often, however, whites join with Republican Latinos to win elections, such as was the case with the election of Mel Martinez to the U.S. Senate in 2004 from Florida. These biracial coalitions often occur in many legislative districts, especially in Democratic primaries.

How do citizens choose between candidates running for office? In many districts, one party dominates the electorate. In these cases, the primary of the dominant party is where the de facto election takes place. This was true in the South for generations, as Democratic primaries picked winners for most of the post–Civil War era (Key 1984). The same dominance explains why Latinos are able to win in districts that are majority-Democratic (Chapter 4 will explore these cases more thoroughly). In many instances, however, citizens do not even have a choice. Because of the strong incumbency effect, many incumbents do not even face major party competition in U.S. House races (Maestas et al. 1999). There is certainly no reason to believe that this is not true at the state legislative level, either, as Gaddie (2004) suggests. Many politicians start their political careers at lower levels and gradually move up the career ladder. In the 103rd Congress, for example, the "percentage of members in state congressional delegations with prior legislative experience averaged 53.3 percent" (Berkman 1994). In most states, the upper chamber is smaller, more exclusive, and often populated by those who previously served in the lower chamber. The preceding discussion leads to the following hypotheses:

District Demography Hypothesis: As the percentage of Latino citizens in a district increase, the probability of electing a Latino to the legislature increases.

Career Paths Hypothesis: A Latino candidate is more likely to be elected to the lower-level chamber than to the upper chamber.

Methods

I test the next set of hypotheses in eight venues – Congress and the state legislatures in New Mexico, California, Texas, Arizona, Florida, New York, and New Jersey. In each case, the unit of analysis is the legislative district, and the analysis is performed for all legislative districts. I conduct the analysis first for the lower house of each legislature in 2003 or 2004. I then replicate the analysis for the two chambers combined (except for Congress and New Jersey, where no Latinos serve in the upper chamber). Where possible, the analysis is also done for each legislature before districts were redrawn for the 2003 or 2004 elections. I chose these states and the Congress because of their geographic and subethnic group diversity in order to rule out region-specific or subethnic group anomalies. Although these seven states also have the largest percentage of Latinos, several states like Colorado, Illinois, and Nevada have recently experienced a surging Latino population and should be explored in future studies.

The dependent variable is whether a district is represented in the legislature by a Latino (Latino coded 1, non-Latino coded 0). The National Association of Latino Elected and Appointed Officials (NALEO) has identified Latino legislators in each chamber. The United States Census Bureau originally collected demographic data. The allocation to legislative districts was done by each state and posted on state-maintained websites. The explanatory variables are the percentage of a given district's population identified in the most recent census as Latino citizens, the percentage of Democrats in the district (or Gore vote for certain states), whether the legislator is an incumbent (1 if incumbent), the median income of the district (for the U.S. House), and the percentage urban in the district (for the U.S. House).[3]

Probit analysis is used to measure the impact of the independent variables on the probability that a district elects a Latino legislator. Probit is the appropriate method for analyzing a dichotomous dependent variable. Since probit coefficients are not as easy to interpret as regression coefficients and to facilitate comparisons across legislatures, I provide tables that show how the probability of electing a Latino candidate varies with the percentage of Latinos in each district (set at 20, 40, 50, 60, and 80 percent, with other variables set at their means).

---

[3] I dropped the percentage of African Americans in a district because there was no significant finding in any of the legislatures. See the appendix for detailed state-by-state analyses that include this variable.

United States House

The percentage of Latinos in the U.S. population stood at 5 percent in 1970. The number had increased to 6 percent in 1980, 9 percent in 1990, and 13 percent in 2000. In the 108th Congress, 22 of the 435 members were Latino (5 percent). Put differently, the proportion of Latinos in Congress in 2004 was equal to the proportion of Latinos in society in 1970.

Do the experiences of Latinos working to win House seats parallel the experiences of African Americans? Canon (1999b), for example, reveals that in "the 6,667 [U.S.] House elections in white majority districts between 1966 and 1996, only 35 (0.52 percent) were won by blacks." Have Latinos done better or worse than this?

In Table 3.1, Latino representative is the dependent variable, and the explanatory variables are identical to those used for the state analyses. Between 1995 and 2003, the number of Latinos serving in the House increased from seventeen to twenty-two, but the analysis demonstrates that the growing Latino population rather than the election of Latinos to non-Latino majority districts has largely fueled this increase. To be sure, Reps. Sires (D-NJ) and Velázquez (D-NY) represent districts that are just shy of a Latino majority. Sires's district is 47 percent Latino while Velázquez' district is 49 percent Latino, with a substantial plurality of African-American voters rendering their districts majority-minority. Chapter 5 explores how these two members of Congress were able to get elected in their districts, as part of a broader analysis of the election of Latino legislators from non-Latino majority districts.

The threshold needed to elect a Latino candidate appears to be much higher in the U.S. House. Districts that are 40 percent Latino have only a 3 percent probability of electing a Latino legislator. It is not until the 60 percent Latino districts that a corresponding 74 percent probability of electing a Latino legislator is reached. Like New York, the U.S. House is a professional legislature with high rates of incumbent re-election. Because many congressional seats are coveted, this makes it difficult for Latinos, who are disproportionately underfunded, to adequately compete, especially against white or African-American incumbents. Most of the Latino legislators with substantial (i.e., 60 percent or above) Latino populations have over 80 percent probability of getting elected to the House. All else equal, Latinos have lower probabilities of getting elected to the U.S. House than they have getting elected to any of the seven state legislatures, except for New York. Majority-Latino districts, as we might

TABLE 3.1. *Probit Analysis of Latino Representation in State Legislatures and the U.S. House*

District	Dependent Variable: Latino Representative = 1						
	AZ	CA	NJ	NM	NY	TX	USH
Percentage Latino Citizen	.123**	.102**	.068*	.060**	.024*	.065**	.228**
	(.046)	(.012)	(.032)	(.013)	(.011)	(.010)	(.078)
Senator Dummy	.087	.165	Coll.	-.303	Coll.	Coll.	–
	(.534)	(.366)		(.336)			
Percentage Gore/ Democratic Vote 2000	.024	-.003	.013	.052**	.032*	.012	-.003
	(.039)	(.013)	(.029)	(.012)	(.012)	(.014)	(.034)
Incumbent	-.322	-.343	–	.668	-1.05*	.013	-2.63
	(.592)	(.369)		(.472)	(.180)	(.517)	(.034)
Median Income							-7.7e-06
							(.000)
Percent Urban							.194*
							(.094)
Constant	-5.3**	-2.99**	-3.17	-5.78**	-3.04**	-3.91**	-24.4*
	(1.65)	(.778)	(1.69)	(1.01)	(1.01)	(.781)	(10.4)
N	90	120	80	112	150	150	425
Pseudo R2	.60	.46	.27	.49	.32	.65	.87

Notes:
*$p<=.05$; **$p<=.01$ (standard errors in parentheses).
@Pfp – predicts failure perfectly.
#Coll.–collinear.
For Florida, data are predicted perfectly.

expect, have strong probabilities electing Latinos. There are a few outliers, including Rep. Howard Berman's (D-CA) district, that are majority-Latino yet continue to elect non-Latino incumbents who have served for long periods, attesting to the continued resilience of the long-observed incumbency advantage in congressional elections (Cox and Katz 1996; Jacobson 1997).

Overall Findings

The strongest predictor for the presence of a Latino in the eight lower chambers studied here is the percentage of Latinos in a legislative district. The probit coefficients for Latino population are large and statistically significant for nearly all legislatures in question. Although it may seem as if all states exhibit similar trends, the differences among the states are remarkable, as the predicted probabilities show.

In the Appendix, probit analyses for six lower chambers just prior to the 2001 redistricting are shown. All six lower chambers exhibit the same substantive results as before. The percentage Latino coefficient is statistically significant in all cases, and the percentage of African Americans in a district is unrelated to the election of Latino candidates. The results cannot be seen as isolated events having to do with how legislative districts were drawn following the 2000 Census because the results indicate that the determinants of the election of Latinos to legislatures are substantively similar.

In the seven state legislatures, we see heavy ethnic and racially based voting among Latinos and African Americans. Regardless of percent African American in district, the best predictor of the presence of Latino legislators is the percentage of Latinos in a district. There appears to be no effect of the upper versus lower chamber on the election of Latino candidates to legislatures neither before nor after redistricting. These overall patterns have not changed in the past ten years, either; they remain identical in all of the states studied in direction and magnitude for the pre-2000 redistricting period. This means that the best way to predict whether a Latino represents a given district is to know the percentage of Latino citizens in such a district.

These findings about Latinos are in line with Grofman and Handley's (1989) observation that the geographical concentration of African Americans is the key factor explaining why there are more African Americans in lower houses than in upper houses. As Latinos assimilate, residential segregation becomes less widespread. As such, Latinos, like

TABLE 3.2. *Probability of a Latino Being Elected to Eight Legislatures,* *2003–2004 Citizens*

Percent Latino Citizen	CA	AZ	NJ	NM	TX	USH	NY
80 percent	99	98	88	97	97	98	36
60 percent	99	95	80	83	76	83	21
50 percent	95	89	72	65	53	40	14
40 percent	77	69	58	42	29	7	9
20 percent	11	5	17	9	3	.4	3

Source: Estimates derived from probit results with all other variables set at their means using CLARIFY®.

many Asian Americans, find their influence diluted by being in districts with white majorities. At the same time, increased assimilation can lead to growing numbers of an ethnic group elected to districts or offices previously unimagined. Italian Americans, Irish Americans, and Jewish Americans currently represent districts and states that have few of their coethnics.[4] This does not mean that their interests are not being represented, but it does mean that it makes it more difficult for Latino candidates to win legislative seats in the short term; the long-term and broader implications are debatable.

The predicted probabilities for seven states and the U.S. House are presented in Tables 3.2 and 3.3. The tables appear identical, but with one major difference: Table 3.3 estimates the probabilities including all Latinos in a district, whereas Table 3.2 estimates the probabilities including only Latino citizens in a district. The legislatures are sorted from highest to lowest probability of electing a Latino at the crucial 50 percent level of Latinos in a district. This ordering is done to assess the electoral responsiveness of these institutions to the presence of Latinos in particular districts. What is perhaps most striking is the extremely high probability of electing a Latino legislator in Florida in a hypothetical district with a 50 percent total Latino population (99 percent probability).[5] Even districts that have a hypothetical 40 percent Latino population have an

---

[4] One can easily think of politicians such as Rudolph Giuliani, Daniel Patrick Moynihan, Edward Kennedy, Russell Feingold, Barbara Boxer, and so on as individuals of Italian, Irish, Jewish, and other backgrounds who represent(ed) constituencies that are (were) not a majority of their ethnic group.

[5] These estimates for Florida are based on an analysis of the percentage of all Latinos in Florida legislative districts. The results are predicted perfectly when considering only the percentage of Latino citizens, making the results even more suggestive of strong descriptive representation.

TABLE 3.3. *Probability of a Latino Being Elected to Eight Legislatures, 2003–2004 All*

Percent Latino	FL	NM	CA	NJ	AZ	TX	NY	USH
80 percent	100	98	95	89	96	87	67	99
60 percent	99	79	71	65	71	52	40	74
50 percent	99	57	50	48	47	31	28	27
40 percent	94	34	30	32	25	15	17	3
20 percent	8	5	5	9	3	2	5	<1

Source: Estimates are derived from probit results using all Latinos in legislative districts, with all other variables set at their means.

extremely high probability (94 percent) of electing a Latino to the Florida legislature. Even at the 20 percent point, the probability of electing a Latino in Florida is 8 percent, which is higher than all but one of the other seven legislatures. Clearly, Florida is the most conducive state to the election of Latinos.

New Mexico, California, New Jersey, and Arizona are all fairly conducive to the election of Latinos at the crucial 50 percent Latino level. These four states have probabilities of electing a Latino ranging from 47 percent to 57 percent. These four states are even more conducive to the election of Latino candidates when only including Latino citizens (ranges from 65 percent to 95 percent). Recall that New Jersey and Arizona have a multimember districting system that previous research has shown to be an institutional barrier to the election of minorities to legislatures (Cartagena 2005; Gerber et al. 1998; Kousser 1992; Welch 1990). On the other hand, research on multimember districts (MMDs) has shown that turnover is slightly higher in these states than in those using single-member districts, thus leading to more open seats (Niemi and Winsky 1987). These findings suggest that in the case of Latinos in New Jersey and Arizona, MMDs are not as harmful as would be expected from previous research.

Texas is one of the least conducive states to the presence of Latinos in legislatures. In a hypothetical 50 percent Latino population district, the probability of electing a Latino is only 31 percent. To be sure, Texas is more responsive to the election of Latino candidates when we control for citizenship, although it is only more responsive than New York or the U.S. House. The Texas Legislature is a citizen legislature that meets for only part of the year, but so is the New Mexico Legislature. Even districts with a 60 percent Latino population have only a 52 percent probability of electing a Latino, making Texas the second least conducive of all seven states at that threshold level, after New York. Despite the political incorporation of Latinos in the Texas Democratic and Republican parties, Latino candidates face more difficulties getting elected in districts with 60 percent and above Latino populations. As more Latinos become Texas voters, these estimates will no doubt change, making Texas an important state to watch in future elections.

New York is one of the least conducive states to the presence of Latinos in legislatures. In a hypothetical 50 percent Latino population district, the probability of electing a Latino is only 28 percent. The probability of a Latino serving in a district with an 80 percent Latino population is 67 percent, which is much lower than in other states. Even in districts with a 60 percent Latino population, the probability of a Latino being elected is 40 percent. Whereas Latinos have been winning in districts with non-Latino majorities throughout the country, this has not been the case in New York. Citizenship does not seem to make matters better in New York, as Table 3.2 demonstrates.

The probability of a Latino being elected to the United States House in a district with a 50 percent Latino population is the lowest at 27 percent (or 14 percent for a 50 percent Latino citizen population). Why is this so? Since Congress is the most prestigious legislative institution available to any candidate, the ability of Latinos to get elected from even near-Latino majority districts is markedly difficult. Since there are no term limits for members of Congress and the prestige is high, there has been remarkably little turnover in seats, and the incumbency advantage is well documented (Cox and Katz 1996). At the same time, however, districts with a solid 60 percent Latino majority have a 74 percent probability of electing a Latino (83 percent probability for 60 percent Latino citizen districts). For the U.S. House, the difference in predicted probabilities between the 50 percent and 60 percent Latino levels is the largest of any legislative institution in this study. This is important for several reasons. First, it demonstrates how sensitive the percentage of Latinos in a district must be to elect Latino legislators. In voting rights litigation, the so-called "65 percent rule" was invoked claiming that districts must be 65 percent African American to elect African Americans. As Swain (1993) and Lublin (1997) argue, this is no longer the case for congressional elections. In the same way, creating 65 percent Latino districts clearly wastes Latino votes. On the other hand, it is also not the case that a 40 or even 45 percent Latino district will have a very high probability of electing Latino legislators. To maximize Latino descriptive representation, districts that are between

55 percent and 60 percent Latino could be created. This does not take into account the tradeoffs regarding substantive representation.

New Mexico

New Mexico, the state with the largest Latino population, is the first state worthy of additional analysis. According to the 2000 Census, 42 percent of the state's population is of Hispanic origin. Unlike other states, many Latinos in New Mexico can trace their lineage back to the Spanish colonial period. For example, current Mayor of Albuquerque Martin J. Chávez traces his lineage back to Spanish colonial settlers.[6] New Mexico has the most Latino statewide officials, including its Governor Bill Richardson. It also has the largest number and the largest percentage of Latino legislators of any state in the country.[7] In 2003, thirty of the seventy legislators in the House were Latino (43 percent), as were fourteen of the forty-two senators (33 percent). New Mexico is not only the most Hispanic state in the country, it is also the only state where the representation of Latinos in one legislative body exceeds the percentage of Latinos in the state population.

Once a part of Mexico, New Mexico was heavily Latino long before it became a state. Indeed, it is the only state in the analysis where the recent growth in Latino population has been relatively modest. In 1970, the state was already 37 percent Latino. It was still 37 percent Latino in 1980, 38 percent in 1990, and 42 percent in 2000. In fact, Latinos with Anglo names, like Governor Bill Richardson, have gone to extraordinary lengths to advertise their Latino heritage. Unlike many other states, New Mexico retained an aristocratic land-owning Latino elite (the "patrones") who have long been involved in state politics. With this long history of Latino political incorporation, it is not surprising that Latinos have done relatively well in state politics, as the analyses below attest.

Although Latinos are better represented in the House (43 percent) than in the Senate (33 percent), the multivariate analysis does not find any significant effects for the upper chamber. The likely explanation for this is that House districts are more numerous and it is therefore easier to create Latino districts for the House than it is for the Senate.

I also replicate the analysis for 1991 to assess the extent to which the election of Latinos to the New Mexico Legislature has changed in the

---

[6] Personal Interview with Mayor Chávez, June 2002, Albuquerque, NM. In fact, one of the Chicano students involved in a group discussion for Latino Ford Fellows remarked that the Mayor did not "look" Mexican.

[7] NALEO 2002 Election Profile (May).

past decade (see Appendix for full results).[8] In that year, twenty-seven of the seventy legislators in the House were Latino (39 percent), as were fourteen of the forty-two legislators in the Senate (33 percent). The findings for 1991 are essentially the same as for 2003. The probit coefficients for the percentage of Latinos in a district are relatively large and the standard errors small so the coefficients are highly significant.

The election of Latino legislators from non-Latino districts is not just a theoretical possibility. Five of the forty-four Latino state legislators in New Mexico were elected from non-Latino districts, including two House members (W. Ken Martínez, D-Grants, and Larry Larrañaga, R-Albuquerque) who were elected from districts with a less than 20 percent Latino population. Chapter 5 analyzes in detail the election of Latino legislators from non-Latino districts.

California

California is the state with the second-highest percentage of Latinos in the country. The state's former Latino Lieutenant Governor, Cruz Bustamante, a Democrat, failed to convince voters to elect him to replace embattled Governor Gray Davis in 2003.[9] In fact, Bustamante's showing among Latino voters was worse than many political observers expected, as Arnold Schwarzenegger won an estimated 30 percent of the statewide Latino vote and State Senator Tom McClintock, a Republican, won 10 percent of the Latino vote. Unlike New Mexico, California's Latino population has been growing rapidly. In 1970, the state was only 14 percent Latino, whereas it was 19 percent Latino in 1980, 26 percent in 1990, and 32 percent in 2000. Baldassare (2002) estimates that by 2040, Latinos will account for 48 percent of the state's population. By 2015, the majority of the state's residents are expected to be either Latino or Asian American. Latino legislators are also numerous in the California legislature.[10] In 1990, the California legislature was comprised of seven Latinos. In 2003, eighteen of the eighty legislators in the Assembly were

---

[8] A change over time variable would be ideal in this case, but the districts are often not composed of the same areas and populations once redistricting takes place. This would make it difficult to compare across time.

[9] Bustamante's bid was damaged by reports that he accepted contributions from Native American casinos and by improper financial record keeping. In addition, his association with the radical group MEChA when he was a college student also hurt his campaign.

[10] The breakdown of California's population by race and ethnicity, according to the 2000 Census, is as follows: 46.7 percent white, 6.4 percent black, 10.8 percent Asian, .5 percent Native American, and 32.4 percent Latino (can be of any race).

Latino (23 percent), as were ten of the forty state senators (25 percent). Latinos have a lower percentage of seats in the House (23 percent) than in the Senate (25 percent).

I also replicate the analysis for 2000 (see Appendix for table). At that time, sixteen of the eighty legislators in the House were Latino (20 percent), whereas nine out of the forty Senators were Latino (23 percent). The analysis for 2000 is virtually the same as for 2003. The probit coefficients for the percentage of Latinos in a district are relatively large, the standard errors small, and the coefficients highly significant.

More than any other state, the probabilities drastically change when we account for citizenship. California is the most responsive to the election of Latinos based on Latino citizenship. A district with a hypothetical 50 percent Latino citizen population had an impressive 95 percent probability of electing a Latino. Even a district with a 40 percent Latino citizen population had a 77 percent probability of electing a Latino. These probabilities show the extent to which *citizenship matters* for Latino political incorporation.

Again, we see that the election of Latino legislators from non-Latino districts was not just a theoretical possibility. Eight of the twenty-seven Latino legislators in California were elected from non-Latino majority districts, including one senator (Deborah Ortíz, D-Sacramento) who was elected from a district that is less than 20 percent Latino. These findings indicate that it is easier for Latinos to win in California than it has been for African Americans (Grofman and Handley 2001). Chapter 5 examines various explanations for how Latino candidates have achieved success in non-Latino districts.

Texas

Texas is the state with the third-largest percentage of Latinos, who compose 32 percent of the population. In 1970, the state was only 18 percent Latino, whereas it was 21 percent Latino in 1980, 26 percent Latino in 1990, and 32 percent Latino in 2000. Although not yet a majority-minority state like California, many scholars estimate that it is only a matter of time before Texas becomes a majority-minority state. In the 2002 elections, Texas Democrats nominated Latino Tony Sánchez for governor and African-American Mayor Ron Kirk of Dallas for the U.S. Senate. Even though both men lost, to Rick Perry and John Cornyn, respectively, it was the first time that Texas Democrats nominated minority candidates for both offices in a single year, indicating the growing power of minorities in the state. In 2008, Democrats in Texas nominated another Latino, State Rep. Rick Noriega (D-Houston), who was unable to match Sen. John Cornyn's fundraising numbers and subsequently met the same fate as previous Democratic hopefuls in Texas's recent elections.

The Texas House includes thirty-one Latinos, or 21 percent of the body, which is substantially below the 32 percent of the state's total Latino population. The Texas Senate includes seven Latino members (23 percent of the body).

The multivariate analysis does not find any significant differences between the two chambers. Recall that in Texas, there are 150 House districts and only 31 Senate districts, which makes it easier for the Legislature to create majority-Latino districts for the House.

The replication of the analysis for 2001, prior to the post-2000 redistricting lines, is also revealing. In that year, 27 of the 150 House legislators were Latino (18 percent), whereas 7 out of the 31 Senators were Latino (23 percent). The analysis for 2001 is also substantively similar to the 2003 analysis. The explanatory power of the 2003 model is slightly stronger.[11] The probit coefficients for the percentage of Latinos in a district are relatively large, the standard errors small, and the coefficients highly significant.

I also show the relationship between the Latino population in a district and the probability that it would elect a Latino legislator. These data are based on the combined House and Senate districts for 2003. Latinos are elected from districts that are not majority-Latino, although the probability of such an event occurring is rather low. Texas, then is fairly unconducive to the election of Latinos. Most of the Latino legislators in Texas come from the Rio Grande Valley and the major cities of Austin, Dallas, Houston, and San Antonio, where geographically concentrated Latino majority districts exist.

When accounting for citizenship, Latinos fare slightly better, but not to the degree of California. A hypothetical 50 percent Latino district has a 53 percent probability of electing a Latino, while a 40 percent Latino district has a 29 percent probability of electing a Latino.

In Texas, three of the thirty-seven Latinos serving in the Legislature in 2003 represented non-majority-Latino districts, including one Latina who was elected from a district with a less than 20 percent Latino population (former Rep. Elvira Reyna, R-Mesquite). In Chapter 5, Reyna's

---

[11] Predicted probability graphs are shown for the 2003–2004 cycles only. Graphs for the preredistricting period are available upon request from the author.

election to the House will be explored along with other Latinos who have been successful in winning in districts that otherwise would not be expected to elect Latinos.

Arizona

Despite being New Mexico's next-door neighbor, the history and politics of Arizona could not be more different. Why is Arizona different, despite its proximity to New Mexico? Immediately prior to the Civil War, when Arizona became independent of New Mexico, Anglo settlers from the Northeast settled in Arizona in large numbers. Along with this settlement came the need to have cheap labor for agricultural work. Mexicans in search of economic opportunity filled these positions. This is different from New Mexico with its long-standing aristocratic "patrones" system dominated by Latinos, which never materialized in Arizona. White settlers became the land-owning elites in the postwar period.

In 1970, Latinos comprised 17 percent of Arizona's population, whereas in 1980, the number dropped to 16 percent, and in 1990 increased to 19 percent. In 2000, Latinos comprised 25 percent of Arizona's population. Unlike New Mexico, however, most Latinos in Arizona generally do not trace their lineage back to Spanish colonial settlers. Because of Arizona's overall growth, two new congressional seats were added following the 2000 Census. Two Latino candidates, George Córdova and Raul Grijalva, competed for separate House seats. Grijalva was elected to the U.S. House. Prior to Grijalva's election, Rep. Ed Pastor of Phoenix, first elected in 1992, had been the only Latino representing Arizona in the U.S. House. In 2003, eleven of the sixty legislators in the House were Latino (18 percent), as were five of the thirty senators (17 percent). More on Arizona's Latino legislators, such as Sen. Jorge García's reflections on his role as a Latino legislator, will be discussed later.

Unlike most other states, Arizona has a multimember districting method of allocating its legislative seats. All ninety legislators are elected from the same thirty districts, with one senator and two members of the Assembly per district. Members are elected in even-numbered years for two-year terms (Berman 1998). One might expect Latinos to have a more difficult time getting elected to the upper chamber, given previous research on the negative impact of multimember districts on the representation of minorities in straight-voting scenarios (Gerber et al. 1998; Kousser 1992; Welch 1990). The multivariate analysis, however, does not find any significant differences between the two houses. Perhaps one reason for this is that Arizona is one of the states to have term limits for legislators, limiting each legislator to eight consecutive years in office. Term limits may have forced long-standing white incumbents to step aside and make room for younger Latinos to win in districts that had become majority or near-majority Latino.[12]

I also replicate the analysis for the preredistricted Arizona Legislature in 2000. In that year, ten of the sixty legislators in the House were Latino (17 percent), as were four of the thirty Senators (13 percent). The analysis for 2000 is substantively the same as for 2003. The probit coefficients for the percentage of Latinos in a district are relatively large, the standard errors small, and the coefficients highly significant.

Like California, citizenship makes a significant difference when it comes to the probability of electing a Latino legislator in Arizona. In a hypothetical 50 percent Latino citizen district, there is an 89 percent probability of electing a Latino. Even a 40 percent Latino citizen district has a 69 percent probability of electing a Latino. Like California, Arizona has a high proportion of undocumented Latino immigrants, which contribute to these differences.

Again, we see that the election of Latino legislators from non-Latino districts was not just a theoretical possibility. Three of the sixteen Latino legislators in Arizona were elected from non-Latino districts, including one senator (Pete Ríos, D-Hayden) who was elected from a district that is 30 percent Latino.[13] Arizona has a lower percentage of Latinos serving in non-Latino majority districts than other states. Chapter 5 examines various explanations for how Latino candidates have achieved success in non-Latino districts, and explains why Arizona is an outlier in this regard.

Florida

The intricacies of Florida politics became national news in November 2000, when George W. Bush and Al Gore became engaged in a bitter fight over who won the 270 electoral votes necessary to win the presidency. Had it not been for an overwhelming turnout among Cuban Americans for Bush, Gore may very well have been elected president, given the razor-thin margin. According to the 1970 Census, Latinos comprised 7 percent

[12] Chapter 4 will discuss in greater detail "near-Latino majority districts," which I define as districts with a Latino population between 45 percent and 49.9 percent.
[13] Arizona's 23rd district is approximately 11 percent Native American.

of Florida's population, whereas in 1980, this percentage had increased to 9 percent of the population. In 1990, Latinos comprised 12 percent of the population, and by 2000, 17 percent of the state's population was Latino. Contrary to popular belief, however, the majority of Florida's Latinos are *not* Cuban American. In fact, Cubans comprise 31 percent of the Latino population, whereas Puerto Ricans comprise 18 percent, Mexican Americans comprise 14 percent, and other groups account for 37 percent.[14] In 2003, 13 of the 120 legislators were Latino (11 percent), as were 3 of the 40 senators (8 percent).

Latino representatives come exclusively from majority-Latino districts, largely in Miami Dade County, but increasingly in the I-4 corridor areas of Tampa and Orlando. I also replicate the analysis for 1996. In that year, 12 of the 120 House members were Latino (10 percent), while 3 of the 40 senators were Latino (8 percent). The analysis for 1996 is similar in many ways to 2003. The percentage of African Americans in a district and whether a legislator is a senator are unrelated to the probability of electing a Latino legislator.

Districts with a tiny Latino population seldom elect a Latino legislator, whereas districts with a 40 percent Latino population had more than a 90 percent chance of electing a Latino candidate.[15] Once a district became majority-Latino, it had an almost perfect chance of electing a Latino legislator. This is the highest level of ethnic-based voting we have seen thus far. Florida is an outlier in that even districts with marginal Latino populations had extremely high probabilities of electing Latino legislators. There are a couple of reasons for this. First, in the Florida Senate, there are no actual districts with a Latino population between 24 and 57 percent. In the Florida House, there are no actual districts with a Latino population between 33 and 49 percent. Latinos currently represent the 33 percent Latino district and the 49 percent Latino district. These results clearly affect the estimates for the hypothetical districts in the mid-range. Unlike most of the other states, once a district is majority-Latino in Florida, the probability of a Latino representation is nearly 100 percent. Florida's Cuban American voters apparently vote heavily along ethnic lines, and their percentage in the population means more in terms of voting power precisely because of higher rates of citizenship, income, and hence voter participation.

---

[14] From United States Census Bureau American FactFinder (http://www.census.gov).
[15] These predictions are based on a different model that can be found in the Appendix.

In Florida, only three of the sixteen Latino legislators represent non-majority-Latino districts (Reps. Bob Henríquez, D-Tampa, John Quiñónes, R-Kissimmee, and Juan Zapata, R-Miami). None of these three representatives is Cuban American, indicating the changing demographics of Florida. Just how these three men were elected, their respective district profiles, and career paths will be explored in Chapter 5 along with other Latino legislators who have been successful in winning in districts that are not majority-Latino.

New York

Many assume that most Latinos in New York live in Spanish Harlem and are of Puerto Rican heritage. Although it is true that most of New York State's Latinos live in New York City, and Puerto Ricans dominated the early immigration of Latinos to the City, later waves were more diverse in their origins and more likely to settle in various parts of the Empire State. For example, migrant workers from Mexico have settled both in New York City and throughout Long Island and the upstate region. In 1970, Latinos of all ethnicities accounted for 8 percent of the population, whereas in 1980, the percentage increased to 10 percent. In 1990, 12 percent of New Yorkers were Latino and in 2000, this percentage had risen to 15 percent. Puerto Ricans comprise 37 percent of the Latino population, Dominicans another 16 percent, Mexican Americans another 9 percent, and Cuban Americans only 2 percent, with the label "other Hispanic" accounting for the remaining 36 percent.[16] Of course, Puerto Ricans still hold most of the political offices among Latinos in New York State. This is because of the group's longer presence in New York and the lower entry costs Puerto Ricans face vis-à-vis other Latinos given their U.S. citizenship. In the New York Legislature, the percentage of Latinos serving in that body has gone from 3 percent in 1986 to 6 percent in 2000.

In 2003, 10 of the 150 members of the New York Assembly were Latino (7 percent), as were 5 of the 62 Senators (8 percent). Like Texas and California, the percentage of Latino state senators in the New York Senate actually exceeds the percentage of Latino representatives in the lower chamber, which is why the results of the multivariate analysis are not as surprising.

---

[16] From United States Census Bureau American FactFinder (http://wwww.census.gov).

Latinos in New York have lower probabilities of getting elected to the Legislature than in other states, like New Mexico. Districts with a tiny Latino population were unlikely to elect Latino legislators, but districts with a 40 percent Latino population had a 17 percent chance of electing Latinos, and districts with a 50 percent population had a 28 percent chance of electing Latinos. Once a district becomes 60 percent Latino, it has a 40 percent chance of electing a Latino legislator.

Unlike California, citizenship numbers tend to skew the results downward. A hypothetical 50 percent Latino citizen district in New York only has a 14 percent probability of electing a Latino. A 40 percent Latino citizen district only has a 7 percent probability. In the Appendix to this chapter, I control for the percentage of African Americans in a district vis-à-vis the election of Latino legislators and African-American legislators. No African-American legislators represent majority-Latino districts in New York, and Latino influence districts (25–49.9 percent Latino) are not significantly related to the election of African-American legislators. Another reason for this finding is that New York's Latino population has a significant plurality of Puerto Rican Latinos, who are U.S. citizens and still have low participation rates, compared to other groups, making these estimates all the more indicative of the potential voting power of Puerto Ricans in New York.

Because of its generous rate of pay, part-time workload, lack of term limits, and incumbent-friendly redistricting, New York's legislature has experienced little turnover in the Legislature in recent years (Stonecash 1993). In a "gentlemen's agreement," legislators have drawn district lines so that the respective parties can retain their majority status in each chamber (Liebschutz 1998). Consequently, the Democratic Party has controlled the General Assembly and the Republican Party had controlled the Senate for more than two decades (until 2006). However, in June 2009, two Latino senators (Hiram Monserrate, D-Queens, and Pedro Espada, D-Bronx) left the Democratic caucus to form a "bipartisan" majority with Republican senators. Some have pointed to possible "black/brown" tension as the reason for this split, given that the majority leader was African American. However, others point to the simple fact that under the deal, Espada became Senate president, which put him in line to serve as governor since the state does not have a lieutenant governor. Between 1991 and 2000, the percentage of turnover in the New York General Assembly and Senate was 14 percent and 11 percent, respectively (Moncrief, Niemi, and Powell 2004). To put these numbers in perspective, only Pennsylvania had a lower turnover percentage during this same time period for the lower chamber, whereas only Delaware and Oklahoma had lower turnover percentages for the upper chamber. All of these factors have made it more difficult for growing ethnic groups to displace entrenched incumbents.

In New York, only one of the fifteen lawmakers in the Legislature represents a non-majority-Latino district (Rep. Phil Ramos, D-Brentwood). No Latino represents a majority-black district, and no evidence of black/brown coalitions are observed in the election of Latinos to the legislature (Casellas 2009b). Assemblyman Felix Ortíz of Brooklyn and Sen. Efraín González of the Bronx represent districts with Latino majorities and offer some reflections on New York's politics in Chapter 4.

New Jersey

Due in large part to its proximity to the major metropolitan centers of the Northeast, New Jersey has become more diverse in recent years. According to the 1970 Census, Latinos made up approximately 4 percent of the state's population. By 1980, Latinos became 7 percent of the population and by 1990, 10 percent of the population. By 2000, this number had increased to 13 percent. New Jersey's Latinos are a diverse group. The Census reports that "Other Hispanics" outnumber Cubans, Puerto Ricans, and Mexicans. Puerto Ricans, however, remain the largest subgroup, followed by Mexican Americans and Cuban Americans. Following James E. McGreevey's election as governor in 2001 and the Democratic takeover of the General Assembly, Albio Sires, a Cuban-born Democrat from West New York, became Speaker of the General Assembly, a first in New Jersey politics.

The New Jersey General Assembly has six Latinos, or 8 percent of the entire body, which is substantially below the 13 percent of Latinos in the state. The State Senate, however, currently has no Latino members. New Jersey also has high levels of "residential segregation between Latinos and non-Hispanic whites" (Cartagena 2005, 15). Prior to his election to the U.S. House in 1992, Bob Menéndez (D) had served as the only Latino in the New Jersey Senate. African Americans account for 13 percent of the population, which is about the same as the percentage of Latinos in the population.

New Jersey has a multimember districting method of electing legislators. In such institutional arrangements, three individuals generally run on a ticket, which leaves more senior politicians running for the Senate seat. Many districts contain large numbers of geographically concentrated African Americans who are more likely to have been mobilized to vote and who have fewer participatory obstacles, such as citizenship and language barriers. This system shows that Latinos are disadvantaged in districts which have a 0–25 percent African-American population. Such districts are significantly *less* likely to have a Latino representative. Despite the fact that New Jersey has five Latino representatives from non-majority-Latino districts, the probability of a Latino getting elected in such Latino plurality districts is no more than 30 percent. This is a striking finding indicating that all five of these Legislators really have surmounted rather daunting institutional obstacles to win and serve in such districts.

Seeking to understand the reasons for how five Latinos have been able to win in New Jersey General Assembly districts, only two of which have combined African-American and Latino majorities, will be the subject of Chapter 5. At a first glance, it does not appear that New Jersey's multi-member districting system alone accounts for this, because if that were the case, we would see similar results in Arizona. Additionally, previous research on multimember districts indicates that they have been benefi-cial for the election of women to legislatures but have been harmful for the election of minorities (Gerber et al. 1998; Nechemias 1987; Swers 2001; Thomas 1991).

Conclusion

What accounts for Latino presence in state legislatures and Congress? Is it just the growth of Latino voters that explains this huge increase, or are Latinos being elected from more heterogeneous districts? So far, the evidence seems to suggest that Latinos are more easily elected from majority-Latino districts, although white voters are more likely to vote for Latino candidates than African-American candidates (Santos and Huerta 2001). As the percentage of African Americans in a district increases, the probability of electing a Latino legislator decreases, although not in a significant way (see Appendix). More black legislators represent majority-Latino districts than Latino legislators represent majority-black districts. Black/brown electoral coalitions are not a reality in any of the legisla-tures, indicating that minority unity is still theoretical (Casellas 2009b, Kaufmann 2003). As Chapter 4 will demonstrate, only three Latino state legislators nationwide represent majority-black districts, and of the sixty-five Latino legislators who represent non-Latino majority districts, fifty-two represent majority-white districts. Latino legislators obviously have the best chances of election in majority-Latino districts, followed by majority-white districts, then majority-minority districts with strong Latino pluralities, and finally majority-black districts.

In most state legislatures and Congress, Latinos are slowly becoming viable contenders in districts that are not majority-Latino. However, the strongest predictor of Latino presence in the legislature remains the percentage of Latino citizens in the district. Florida is unlike any other state in this study in that the threshold for the ability of Latinos to get elected more than 90 percent of the time is at the low 40 percent Latino population level. On the other hand, the U.S. House is the chamber with the most difficult prospects for Latino candidates. The ability of Latinos to get elected in New York's highly professional legislature is also relatively difficult, regardless of citizenship status.

Each state has unique characteristics, but as Lublin (1997) shows for the U.S. House, the "probability of a non-Latino gaining election in a Latino majority district declines as the percentage of Latinos in a district rises" (49). This chapter certainly corroborates this finding for state legislatures, yet Latinos are also increasingly being elected to non-Latino majority districts in state legislatures. Unlike Congress, Latino candidates have become more competitive in non-Latino majority districts. This bodes well for future Latino politicians in that more Latinos will be elected to districts with sizeable Latino population, not to mention Latino majority districts. The implications for this increased descriptive representation on the substantive policy issues that Latinos care about seems positive in that a recent study for African Americans in legislatures indicates that African-American interests have been promoted with the growing numbers of African Americans in legislatures (Haynie 2001).

These findings can be explained in part by the effect of term limits and the baseline success of incumbents running for re-election. Of the seven legislatures in this study, Arizona, Florida, and California have enacted term limits after 1992. The adoption of term limits apparently has had unintended positive consequences for the election of Latinos to legislative bodies. Florida is the most conducive state in this study, largely because 56 percent of the lower chamber were new members in 2000, the year term limits went into effect. In the upper chamber, 35 percent were new members, mainly because of the staggered terms in that body. If New York and Texas want more responsive legislatures, then the implementation of term limits would no doubt increase the probabilities of electing more Latinos.

Arizona's responsiveness levels may be stunted by the presence of the MMD system that has been shown to be harmful to the election of minorities (Kousser 1992; Welch 1990). Coupled with term limits, the result in Arizona has been for legislators to move from one body to the next. In 2002, eleven members of the sixty-member Arizona House moved to the Senate. Because members of the lower chamber have the same constituency as the upper chamber, the effect of term limits in Arizona remains to be seen. Taken together, however, turnover rates have been on a downward trend in non-term-limited states, which is partly explained by high rates of incumbent re-election success (Moncrief, Niemi, and Powell 2004).

Chapter 6 will discuss in further detail the effects of Latino descriptive representation on the way Latino members of Congress and legislators behave in roll call settings. In other words, do Latinos, once in office, vote differently than non-Latinos? Additionally, what is the impact, if any, of the Latino voting population on the roll call voting patterns of representatives? The next chapter, however, focuses on how Latino legislators view themselves in terms of perceptions of representation, issue priorities, and the relative importance of descriptive representation.

4

Electing Latinos in Non-Latino Majority Districts

"But we are different from Latinos in places like Texas, Florida, and California because we are extremely new to the state. We do not have an established Latino middle class."

– Sen. Jarrett Barrios (D-Boston)[1]

What accounts for the election of Latinos to districts in which Latinos are not a majority? Are Latinos elected primarily in majority-African-American districts or majority-white districts? Are Latinos winning by appealing to the Latino pluralities in their districts and then adding the minimum number of non-Latino voters? Are Latinos defeating incumbents? If so, are they white or African-American incumbents? Are they winning in multicandidate primaries? Do Latinos with Anglo names appear to have an advantage? To what extent has each political party been responsible for the growing number of Latinos elected in non-Latino majority districts? To what extent have features of the electoral system contributed to more Latino victories in such districts? Now that Latinos have become the largest minority group in the United States, it is fitting to examine the conditions under which Latinos are elected to legislative bodies. In particular, this chapter seeks to explore the conditions under which Latinos are elected to non-Latino majority districts. I argue that although demographics play an important role in the election of Latino candidates, we must look beyond the obvious Latino majority districts that elect Latino legislators. The growing mainstreaming of Latinos in

---

[1] Sixth Annual Harvard Latino Law and Policy Conference: Latino Leadership and Collective Power, April 2003.

American society is already manifesting itself in the election of Latino legislators in areas where traditionally they are not likely to be elected.

For African Americans, election to Congress and state legislatures in non-African-American majority districts has occurred, although not at levels that please many civil rights activists. Some African-American members of Congress are elected from districts with combined African-American and Latino majorities, such as Charles B. Rangel (D-NY), Maxine Waters (D-CA), and Laura Richardson (D-CA). However, as Grofman et al. (1992) show, white voters become less likely to vote for African-American candidates as the proportion of African Americans in a district increases. Martin Kilson (2002) notes "since the 1960s, only a few African-American congressional officeholders have gained office through majority support from white voters." He identifies Senator Edward Brooke (R-MA), who served from 1967 to 1979, Senator Carol Moseley-Braun (D-IL), who served from 1993 to 1996, and Congressman J. C. Watts (R-OK), who served from 1995 to 2003. In addition, Congressman Gary Franks (R-CT) represented a majority-white district from 1991 through 1997. In the current Congress, only four of the thirty-seven members of the Congressional Black Caucus represent majority-white districts. These four districts are represented by Barbara Lee (D-CA), Sanford Bishop (D-GA), Andre Carson (D-IN), and Melvin Watt (D-NC). Even though these four districts are majority-white, since 1992, redistricting commissions or legislatures have increased the percentage of blacks in these districts to make it easier for the black incumbents to get re-elected. Classic redistricting politics involve protecting incumbents, regardless of race. Nevertheless, under *Bush v. Vera*, using race as the predominant factor in redistricting is unconstitutional even when protecting incumbents is a key factor. Seven of the thirty-seven African-American legislators represent districts that are majority-minority, although not majority-African American.

African Americans have achieved most of their gains in legislative races through the elite-driven process of redistricting. At least initially, Democratic leaders supported the creation of majority-minority districts to elect minority Democrats and achieve the desirable effect of having "more black faces in high places." More recently, some Democratic leaders and political scientists have argued that the creation of majority-minority districts has been harmful to the interests of African Americans primarily because packing minority voters into a very few districts has the consequence of electing more Republicans in neighboring districts that have fewer minority voters (Cameron et al. 1996; Canon 1999a; Lublin 1997;

Swain 1995). In an unexpected turn, Republicans have filed lawsuits on behalf of disenfranchised minority voters arguing in favor of the creation of majority-minority districts precisely because such districts increase the probability of electing Republicans to the more strongly majority-white districts (*Page v. Bartels*).

Although Latinos have no doubt benefited from redistricting just like African Americans, Latinos have also been successfully elected to districts with non-Latino majorities. Why is it, then, that Latinos have been elected to sixty-five non-Latino majority districts? What accounts for the election of Latinos to districts in which they have no clear advantage?

Latinos, like any other challengers to incumbents, are more likely to have first been elected to legislative seats in open seat contests. The incumbency advantage is as strong in state legislative races as it is in congressional races (Cox and Katz 1996; Jacobson 1997). Ten of the sixty-five Latinos who represent non-Latino majority districts were first elected to seats in multicandidate primaries, indicating some competition. Six of the sixty-five Latinos challenged other minorities for seats in the general election. Governors or other party leaders initially appointed a smaller number to their seats. Those who do not win in open seat races often defeat white or African-American incumbents who have seen their districts grow in terms of the Latino population, and if incumbents lose, they often do so in the Democratic primaries. Discovering precisely how Latinos are able to win in non-Latino majority districts will be the subject of the rest of this chapter.

Methodology

This section explains the methods used to create the lists of legislators and the sources used to determine the identity of state legislators and their corresponding district composition. It also explains the criteria used to sort Latino legislators into the different categories discussed later in this chapter. I conclude with some reflections as to why this approach is crucial for the understanding of the election of Latinos to Congress and state legislatures, and outline how future research projects could test many of the hypotheses more systematically.

The National Association of Latino Elected and Appointed Officials (NALEO) publishes an annual roster of Latino elected officials throughout the United States. I have used its data to identify Latino state legislators and members of Congress. To determine the racial and ethnic composition of each district, I have examined data posted on state-maintained

TABLE 4.1A. *Latino Representatives in the United States, 2004*

	Number of Latino Representatives		
	Majority-Latino Districts	Non-Latino Majority Districts	Total
Seven States	132	27	159
Forty-Three States	25	36	61
U.S. House	20	2	22
Total	177	65	242

Source: 2004 NALEO Directory of Latino Elected Officials and U.S. Census Bureau Public Law 94–171 Redistricting Data for state legislatures and the *Almanac of American Politics* for U.S. House.

websites. The data were originally collected by the U.S. Census Bureau. I allocated the data to legislative districts by each state by examining data posted on state-maintained websites. For states with little or no relevant information on their websites, I contacted the State Legislature directly and obtained the appropriate data. The demographic variables are the percentage of a given district's population identified in the most recent census as Latino or African American.[2] For all Latino state legislators, I identify which district they represent in the appropriate legislature and determine the percentage of Latinos in their district by consulting Census Public Law 94–171 Redistricting data.

This process involves a very clear selection on the dependent variable, and the reasons for doing so are intentional and warranted. First, this is an exploratory analysis. A more comprehensive research design would require the collection of data on all state legislative districts nationwide. Because extensive district-level data is difficult to obtain, this project would require extensive research. The analysis in this chapter nonetheless prepares the ground for future research. It gives rise to testable hypotheses to explain the success of Latino candidates in non-Latino majority districts. Future research can test these hypotheses with a nationwide district-level comprehensive database.

What kinds of districts elect Latino legislators? Table 4.1a shows all Latino representatives in the United States serving in 2004.[3] In the seven states discussed in more detail in the previous chapter, 132 Latino

---

[2] Unless specifically stated, the percentage Latino and African American figures include the entire population.

[3] This list does not include Latinos elected in November 2004.

TABLE 4.1B. *African-American Representatives in the United States, 2004*

	Number of African-American Representatives		
	Majority-Black Districts	Non-Black Majority Districts	Total
Seven States	51	44	95
Forty-Three States	411	97	508
U.S. House	25	12	37
Total	487	153	640

Source: 2004 Joint Center for Political and Economic Studies and U.S. Census Bureau Public Law 94–171 Redistricting Data for state legislatures and the *Almanac of American Politics* for U.S. House.

legislators represent majority-Latino districts, whereas only 27 Latino legislators represent non-Latino majority districts. In the remaining forty-three states, twenty-five Latino legislators represent majority-Latino districts, whereas thirty-six Latino legislators represent non-majority-Latino districts. This ratio is lopsided because the majority of Latino legislators reside in the seven states detailed in Chapter 3. To the extent that Latinos have been elected in the remaining forty-three states, it is largely in non-Latino majority districts. In the United States House, twenty Latino members of Congress represent majority-Latino districts, whereas only two Latino members of Congress represent non-Latino majority districts. In all, sixty-five Latino legislators represent non-Latino majority districts across the country. Precisely how these Latinos were able to win in such districts forms the basis for this chapter.

How does the election of Latinos compare to the election of African-American legislators? Table 4.1b shows African-American representatives in the United States serving in 2004. For purposes of comparison, this table is shown to demonstrate that, although there are more than twice the number of African-American legislators than Latino legislators in the United States, only 153 out of 640 (24 percent) represent non-African-American majority districts. Many of these districts, however, have combined African-American and Latino majorities. In the U.S. House, only three African Americans currently represent majority-white districts (Reps. Sanford Bishop, D-GA, Gwen Moore, D-WI, and Andre Carson, D-IN), whereas the remaining nine represent majority-minority districts.[4] Latino legislators representing non-Latino majority

[4] The late Representative Julia Carson, D-IN, also represented a majority-white district.

districts represent only a slightly higher percentage (27 percent). The bulk of African-American legislators are elected from majority-African-American districts, which comprise 487 out of 640 districts (76 percent).

Notice that the number of majority-African-American districts is more than twice the number of majority-Latino districts. This is due to several factors. First, redistricting schemes initially created majority-African-American districts at a time when the Latino population was less influential. Secondly, the African-American population is more residentially segregated and concentrated in urban areas, which makes it easier to draw legislative districts that have majority-African-American populations. As Latinos assimilate into whiter neighborhoods, the ability to form legislative districts with Latino majorities becomes much more difficult. Finally, majority-African-American districts created in the 1970s and 1980s, for example, cannot technically be dismantled because of the Voting Rights Act of 1965 and subsequent renewals. However, through redistricting, some of these districts have become less homogenous, thus diluting minority voting strength.

Subsequent tables in this chapter divide Latino legislators into several categories based on district composition, personal characteristics, or the circumstances that led to their election to the legislature. I interviewed some but not all of these legislators (see Chapter 5) to ascertain pertinent points about their political backgrounds and perceptions of representation. The following discussion explains the procedures and methods used to sort these legislators. Table 4.2 lists six Latino candidates who were opposed by other minority candidates in the general election when they were first elected. I obtained this information with the help of Lexis-Nexis searches, local newspaper accounts, secretary of state websites, and candidate websites. I used the same searches to obtain information for Tables 4.3, 4.4, and 4.8 on the initial circumstances that brought Latinos to legislative office, including whether they were appointed, recruited by party leaders, or candidates in multicandidate primaries. Table 4.5 shows Latino legislators with Anglo names. This table was produced by examining the family names of all Latino legislators in this database and determining which names were not of Hispanic origin. That is, Census Public Law 94–171 redistricting data is used to determine which Latino legislators represent districts that are near a Latino majority and those that have combined African-American and Latino majorities. Some Latino legislators are listed in two tables. For example, some legislators represent near-Latino majority districts (Table 4.6) that also have combined

African-American and Latino majorities (Table 4.7). In these cases, the final column in each table indicates whether a particular legislator is also listed in another table.

The Elite-Driven Process

African Americans made major gains in legislatures when redistricting created majority-African-American districts. Although Latinos have certainly benefited from similar redistricting efforts, Latino candidates have also benefited from other ways that elites have made the playing field more hospitable to their political careers. Elites in both parties can do a variety of things to help minorities win in non-minority districts. For example, two minority candidates can run against each other, thus ensuring the election of a minority. Additionally, in some states, governors can make appointments to vacant legislative seats until the next regular election, which can give Latino legislators the benefit of incumbency as they try to win the following election. In addition, party leaders can actively recruit and fund qualified Latino candidates to run in districts.

Redistricting

Redistricting battles are often in the news because they represent politics in its purest form. Politicians of both parties attempt to redraw legislative lines to maximize the number of seats their party can win in elections. In this process, the end often justifies the means. Republicans sometimes become protectors of majority-minority districts to create even more safe Republican seats. Democrats are sometimes willing to effectively end the career of some minority incumbents for the greater partisan good. Sometimes, state legislators cannot agree on a plan, and the courts ultimately decide how districts should be drawn.

Like many others, the Texas State Legislature could not agree on a map in 2001; traditionally, the House Speaker appoints a Redistricting Committee made up of Democrats and Republicans. Democratic Speaker Pete Laney named Delwin Jones, a Republican, the chair of the committee as a symbolic gesture of bipartisanship. The committee's task was to develop a map that was consistent with the Voting Rights Act and existing case law on redistricting. If members were unable to produce a mutually agreeable map, then the Legislative Redistricting Board was mandated to draw the lines (Riddlesperger 2003). Ultimately, in *Balderas et al v. Texas*, the U.S. District Court set districts for the 2002 elections.

In 2003, Republicans grew angry at the court-drawn districts because they felt they could redraw districts that would expand their majorities in the U.S. House. As Riddlesperger (2003) pointed out, however, Republicans did not object to the State Legislature plans, but rather to the U.S. House map. The story behind the story is that Rep. Tom DeLay, then-Majority Leader of the U.S. House, was the driving force behind this plan. DeLay's House majority was delicate, and given the perceived closeness of the 2004 election, adding several new Texas Republicans to the U.S. House delegation could offset losses in other parts of the country. Many Democratic members of the Texas Legislature fled the state during the session in order to protest the proposed redistricting plan. This in effect prevented a quorum, which forced Governor Rick Perry (R) to call a special session to address the issue of redistricting. The issue became a national controversy in which Democrats accused Republicans of playing politics and disenfranchising minority voters (Bickerstaff 2007). Ultimately, a plan that experts say benefits Republicans did pass the Legislature and was cleared by John Ashcroft's Justice Department as being consistent with the Voting Rights Act of 1965.

Like Texas, New Jersey's redistricting process also resulted in litigation. New Jersey has an Apportionment Commission composed of five Democrats and five Republicans appointed by their respective state party chairs. Their task is also to develop a map consistent with the Voting Rights Act and redistricting case law. If the ten members are unable to produce a mutually agreeable map, then the Chief Justice of the New Jersey Supreme Court appoints a nonpartisan eleventh member. The Apportionment Commission has generally failed to agree on a map. In 1991, the then-Chief Justice of the New Jersey Supreme Court appointed Donald Stokes, a professor of public affairs and politics at Princeton University, as the nonpartisan member. In 2001, not coincidentally, Chief Justice Deborah Poritz appointed the Stokes Professor of Public Affairs and Politics at Princeton University, Larry M. Bartels, to serve on this commission. Bartels ultimately sided with the Democrats, which prompted many Republicans to file a lawsuit alleging a violation of the Voting Rights Act's provision to ensure minority voting rights in Newark. The redistricting plan was ultimately upheld by the courts.

Redistricting battles in Texas and New Jersey show just how much is at stake in redistricting. In both states, the number of majority-minority districts has been a matter of partisan dispute. This process has ignited the debates over descriptive and substantive representation and the relative importance of each type (Lublin 1997; Mansbridge 1999;

Swain 1995). Even among elites in the Latino community, there is no consensus as to which type is more important. Congressman Silvestre Reyes (D-TX), former chair of the Congressional Hispanic Caucus, has indicated his clear support for substantive over descriptive representation. He would rather support incumbent white members of Congress than risk a divisive primary, perhaps referring to Diana DeGette's Denver district in which a Latina challenged her in the Democratic primary in a 54 percent minority district (Wallison 2001). On the other hand, Larry González of the NALEO believes that the Congressional Hispanic Caucus is simply neglecting what should be its apparent goal – the election of more Latinos to Congress. Chapter 6 will discuss in further detail the impact of increased descriptive representation on the substantive representation of Latinos.

Two Minority Candidates

Sometimes, minority candidates run in the same district, thus guaranteeing the election of a minority legislator. This can come about in various ways. Political parties can influence the process by adjusting their strategies according to the competitive nature of the district. In some one-party-dominated districts, the dominant party may take a risk and nominate a minority candidate who has a strong probability of winning the general election. On the other hand, the weaker party can also nominate a minority candidate to demonstrate its commitment to the minority community. Alternatively, both political parties may run minorities against each other, especially in districts with strong pluralities of each ethnic group.

As Table 4.2 shows, six of the sixty-five Latinos elected in non-Latino majority districts fall into this category, including four Democrats and two Republicans. The Democrats not discussed include a Dominican representative from Connecticut, a Puerto Rican representative from New York, and a Mexican-American representative from California. These representatives come from safe Democratic districts, and their challengers were either Asian American (in the case of the California representative) or other Latinos. This indicates that for the most part, Latinos are not competing with other minorities to win their legislative seats. On the contrary, Latinos have defeated white candidates in fifty-nine of the sixty-five districts. Latinos are not fighting over "minority" legislative seats, but instead are winning in white-majority areas from Idaho to Georgia.

In Florida, the quintessential battleground state, it should be no surprise that there are also battleground districts with competitive elections.

TABLE 4.2. *Two Minority Candidates in General Election*

Winner	Party	State	Opponent	Ethnicity	Also in Table
Henríquez, Bob	D	FL	Deborah Tamargo	Latina	
Machado, Michael	D	CA	Alan Nakanishi	Asian American	
Pacheco, Bob	R	CA	Ben Wong	Asian American	
Quiñónes, John	R	FL	José Fernández	Latino	
Ramos, Phil	D	NY	Phil Goglas	Latino	4.7
Reinoso, Felipe	D	CT	José Quiroga	Latino	4.7

Bob Henríquez is a fourth-generation Latino whose great-grandfather was mayor of West Tampa. A graduate of Princeton University, he served his community by coaching football for Tampa Catholic High School. He was also a senior planner with the local Planning and Growth Management Commission and was a lobbyist for the Builder's Association of Greater Tampa. He decided to challenge a freshman Republican in 1998 in West Tampa, which has 45,000 registered Latino voters (16 percent of the district's population). African Americans comprise another 16 percent of the district's voting population. In 2002, Latino Republican Héctor Vila challenged him by suggesting, among other things, that he "would communicate with his constituents better than the incumbent does," alluding to the fact that Henríquez was not fluent in Spanish. (Lengell n.d.). Vila, however, was unsuccessful in his bid, given that the district was heavily Democratic, despite the fact that it was about 32 percent minority and thus majority-white.

Henríquez has been named by the Democratic Leadership Council (DLC) as one of the 100 state and local Democrats to watch. His moderate voting record has earned him the endorsement of the *St. Petersburg Times*, whose editorial board claims "his sound approach to lawmaking is also an antidote to heightened partisanship in the House. He has moved the Democrats toward the center on issues, such as education and the environment, which transcend ideology, making his minority party heard" (Editorial 2000). To the extent that a Democrat can be elected in a majority-white district in the South, Henríquez has been able to appeal to African Americans and Latinos, but most importantly to whites, who ultimately determine the winner in this district.

Elected as the first Puerto Rican Republican to the Florida House in 2002, John Quiñónes is seen by many national Republicans as the segue for Republican victories in gubernatorial, senatorial, and presidential elections.[5] His district is 32 percent Latino and 11 percent African American, which makes it still majority-white, but the Latino population in this Orlando-based district is largely Puerto Rican. It is a swing district in which former Vice President Al Gore won 60 percent of the vote in 2000, whereas Florida Governor Jeb Bush won the district by smaller margins twice. Because Florida has become a battleground state, there is no question that this district will continue to be heavily targeted by the political parties. In 2002, Quiñónes beat José Fernández, a Nicaraguan-born Democrat, to win this competitive seat in a campaign that touted his identity as "John Q," which some Democrats believe was aimed at attracting white votes (Stein 2003). Because Republicans were interested in keeping Quiñónes, he was the only freshman Republican to chair a committee in the House of Representatives. Democrats and Republicans in Florida have actively recruited Latino candidates to run in competitive districts. Both parties recognize the importance of Latino voters in determining the outcome of the election in both districts and have thus tried to display their Latino candidates.

Sometimes, however, Latinos may be elected to office despite the efforts of the party establishment. Assemblyman Bob Pacheco, a Mexican-American Republican, was first elected in 1998 to represent a district that is 24 percent Latino and majority-white. He narrowly defeated Democrat Ben Wong by a 52–45 percent margin. Prior to his election, Pacheco served as a business advisor and attorney, a bank vice president, and an owner of a manufacturing company in what is undoubtedly a successful career. He is the chair of the Latino Republican caucus and is active in recruiting Latino voters and candidates to the Republican Party of California. Pacheco describes his initial election to the Assembly by saying that he "was a dark horse..." and that "the party endorsed [his] opponent" (Rojas 2003). In this case, two minority candidates ran against each other, *despite* the fact that Pacheco was not the desired candidate of his party elite. In the end, white Republicans supported a Latino Republican instead of an Asian Democrat.

By running two minority candidates, both political parties effectively guarantee the election of minority candidates. Nonetheless, no case in my dataset involves an African American running against a Latino. This is true even in the Connecticut and New York districts that have combined

---

[5] Due to term limits, Representative Quinónes stepped down in 2006 and was replaced by a Puerto Rican Democrat. He currently serves as the County Commissioner, a more prestigious post in Florida.

TABLE 4.3. *Latino Legislators First Appointed to Seat*

Name	Party	State	Also in Table
Aguilar, Ray	R	NE	4.4
Cruz-Pérez, Nilsa	D	NJ	
Esquivel, Sal	R	OR	
Gutiérrez-Kenney, Phyllis	D	WA	
Martínez, Elmer	D	ID	

African-American and Latino majorities. Henríquez's Florida district has a 16 percent African-American population, but an African-American Democrat would stand a lower probability of winning than a white Democrat in a Southern white-majority district. Quiñónes's Florida district has a much smaller African-American population, and the Democrats can only be competitive running Puerto Rican Democrats. Latinos seem to be in tension with other Latinos and with Asian Americans rather than with African Americans for seats in California legislatures.

Appointment to Vacancies

Another elite-driven way affecting Latino representation in state legislatures involves the use of the appointment power by chief executives of states and party committees to boost Latino representation. In many states, governors can appoint whomever they wish to fill vacancies in the state legislature. Sometimes, governors must choose someone from the same political party as the previous office holder. In some states, county commissioners appoint individuals to serve out terms in the State House or Senate. Of the Latinos serving in non-Latino majority districts, five were initially appointed to their seats (see Table 4.3). This is an effective way for political amateurs to instantly acquire the advantages of incumbency, including increased name recognition and access to more campaign funds, either from their party or special interest groups (Cox and Katz 1996; Jacobson 1997).

Initially appointed to the House in 2001 by Republican Governor Dirk Kempthorne, Elmer Martínez represents an Idaho district with 10 percent Latino population and less than 1 percent African-American population. Democrat Bert Marley, who was chosen by Governor Kempthorne to fill a vacancy in the Senate, had vacated his seat. Kempthorne chose Martínez after reviewing the files of two other candidates – both Democrats. By law, the governor must appoint a member of the same political party to a vacant state legislative seat. He is a Pocatello native and served in the fire department for twenty-five years prior to his appointment. In 2002, Martínez ran for re-election unopposed in the Democratic primary, and against Republican Vern Tilton in the general election, whom he defeated by a 53–47 percent margin.

Senator Ray Aguilar (R) was appointed to the Nebraska Legislature in 1999 by Republican Governor Mike Johanns to replace Chris Peterson who resigned to take a position in the governor's cabinet. Aguilar's district has a 16 percent Latino population and less than 1 percent African-American population. In 2000, Aguilar ran for the seat and was elected to a full term in the Legislature by a wide margin. Since he is the only Latino serving in Nebraska's Legislature, the state Republican party has been active using Aguilar to appeal to the state's small Latino population.

Senator Sal Esquivel (R) represents a district in Oregon with an 8 percent Latino population and a less than 1 percent African-American population. He was originally elected to the Medford City Council in 1997, where he served until he was appointed by the county commissioners to serve out the remainder of Len Hannon's term in the Oregon Senate. Unlike other states, the governor of Oregon (Democrat Ted Kulongoski) was not involved in the selection of Esquivel. Esquivel, however, decided to run for a State House seat in 2004 instead of election to the Senate seat.

Assemblywoman Nilsa Cruz-Pérez (D) made history by becoming the first Latina elected to serve in the New Jersey Legislature. Born in Puerto Rico, she moved to New Jersey in 1991 as part of an assignment with the U.S. Army. In 1995, she was appointed to take the seat of Assemblyman Wayne Bryant, who was appointed to the State Senate that year. Her district is rather diverse, with the 17 percent Latino population and the 25 percent African-American population. She subsequently has been re-elected on a ticket with fellow Assemblyman Joe Roberts.

Representative Phyllis Gutiérrez –Kenney (D) represents a majority-white district in Northern Seattle. She grew up in Montana as the daughter of Mexican farm workers and moved to Seattle when she was five years old. Her district has a 5 percent Latino and 4 percent African-American population, although Seattle is known for its progressive white voters. She began her political career by running for Secretary of State in 1996 against Republican Ralph Munro, who defeated her by a significant margin. She was later appointed to her House seat in 1997 and was elected to a full term shortly thereafter, defeating Republican Don Arnold by a 77–23 percent margin. She has subsequently been re-elected with either no opposition or no serious challenges.

Other than having been appointed, what do these five individuals have in common? After all, these five legislators include representatives, senators, Democrats, Republicans, Easterners, Westerners, and Midwesterners. This could not be a more internally diverse group. All of these districts have less than 17 percent Latino population, whereas the African-American population in all districts but one is less than 4 percent. All of these districts except Martínez's, however, are heavily partisan in one direction or another. As such, the appointer really took little risk in appointing a Latino for fear of losing the seat for his party. In fact, Governor Kempthorne (R-ID) could take the credit for appointing a Latino, but in the end, the Anglo Republican who later ran against Martínez lost by a narrow margin. One thing is clear – being appointed to a seat automatically confers an incumbency advantage. All of the individuals in this sample who ran for re-election won.

Recruitment of Latinos by Party Leaders

Another example of how party elites have helped bring about Latino representation is by recruiting candidates to run in open seats or against weak incumbents. Several strategies can be pursued in this vein. First, Latinos can be identified and recruited to run in districts that are so strongly partisan that their probability of winning is almost certain. This ensures that their party maintains control of that legislative seat. On the other hand, party leaders may recruit a talented Latino candidate to run in a highly competitive district with a strong Latino plurality to increase the probability of winning. As Table 4.4 shows, party leaders classify five of the sixty-five Latinos representing non-Latino majority districts as recruits. In this case, they are all Republican legislators handpicked to demonstrate the party's commitment to the Latino community.

Falling into the first category just described, Senator Tom Apodaca (R-Henderson, NC) is a Baptist who is married with two children. He settled in North Carolina from El Paso, Texas. He began his political career by being recruited by local Republican Party officials to run for the open Senate seat in his district. This new district had less than 1 percent Latino population and a 24 percent African-American population. Apodaca, however, ran as a "white" candidate in that he acknowledged the fact that "I've never considered myself Hispanic. But I've never considered myself not Hispanic" (Rice 2002). He also makes clear that he is not interested in pursuing a "Hispanic agenda," but instead wants to advocate Republican ideas regardless of race.

TABLE 4.4. *Latino Legislators Recruited by Party Leaders*

Name	Party	State	Also in Table
Aguilar, Ray	R	NE	4.3
Apodaca, Tom	R	NC	
Casas, David	R	GA	
Goico, Mario	R	KS	
Maldonado, Abel	R	CA	

Representative David Casas is a Cuban American who was born in the Canary Islands to Cuban parents. He arrived in the United States at two years old, however, and grew up in Georgia, attending Georgia State University and teaching high school civics and history. In 2002, he was elected to his first term in Georgia's General Assembly. He was unchallenged in the Republican primary and soundly defeated a Libertarian opponent in the general election in a district with a 13 percent Latino population and a 16 percent African-American population. In white Georgia, Democrats apparently do not even bother to run for some offices. In Casas' case, the Republicans wanted to nominate someone who they could tout as a Latino among their ranks. This was all the more important that year, when two other Latinos were elected to the Georgia Legislature for the first time ever.

Apodaca and Casas exemplify the Republican Party's efforts to bring Latino elected officials into their ranks in the Deep South. Outside of the South, Republicans have recruited Latinos from Dominican and Puerto Rican backgrounds (González, R-NH, and Garcia, R-CA), but in the South, the successful Republican candidates have been elected from majority-white districts as "white" candidates. In this sense, skin color matters in that white voters are willing to welcome Latinos into their "fold" just as they welcomed Italians, Irish, and other ethnics in the nineteenth century (Glazer 1998). The Democratic Party, however, has not actively pushed Latino candidates to run in districts that are not majority-Latino. There are several possible reasons for this. First, the Democratic Party does not need to tout Latino candidates because most Latino legislators are already members of the Democratic Party. Secondly, the Democratic Party may not want to risk endorsing a Latino candidate over an African-American candidate for fear of the perception of favoring one minority group over another. Finally, few majority-white heavily Democratic districts remain outside of the Northeast and the West Coast, making it all the more difficult for Latinos to be recruited by party leaders to run.

Features of the Electoral System

The preceding discussion has largely focused on how party leaders and organizations have been able to influence the selection of candidates running for legislative seats. Whereas Latinos and African Americans have benefited from redistricting, appointments to empty seats, and focused recruitment efforts, many Latinos have managed to get elected to legislative seats without the help of elites.

Candidates Not Obviously Latino

In some districts, Latino candidates with notably Anglo names have been elected to districts that are not majority-Latino. These individuals may be Latinas who have taken on their white husbands' names, or Latinos who have Latina mothers, like Governor Bill Richardson (D-NM). The strategies that politicians pursue with regard to their Anglo names, however, do vary. In some cases, Latinos do not wish to be identified as such in majority-white districts for fear of being less competitive in the primary and/or general election. As Table 4.5 shows, eleven of the sixty-five Latinos representing non-Latino majority districts have Anglo names. Of the eleven, six are Democrats and five are Republicans. Seven of the eleven in this category are Latinas. Overall, only 11 of the 157 Latino legislators from majority-Latino districts have Anglo family names, indicating that the use of not obviously Latino names is much higher in districts without Latino majorities.[6]

Representative Fran Coleman (D-CO) represents a district with 33 percent Latino population and 2 percent African-American population in the Denver area. She was first elected in 1998 in a hotly contested open seat race, which she won by a narrow margin. In 2000, she defeated her Republican opponent by a much more comfortable margin, and in 2002, she ran unopposed for her seat. She has assumed her husband's family name, so many voters in her district may be unaware that she is a Latina, which probably does not hurt her in this majority-white district in Denver.

Like Coleman, Representative Tom Sawyer (D-KS) is a Latino who has a Mexican mother and an Anglo father. He first ran for county treasurer in 1984, a race in which the person he lost to died the following

---

[6] Candidates can use their names strategically. For example, candidates with Anglo last names might use their Latino first names if they deem this practice to be electorally beneficial.

TABLE 4.5. *Latino Legislators with Anglo Names*

Name	Party	State	Also in Table
Butcher, Dorothy	D	CO	
Coleman, Fran	D	CO	
Frommer, Dario	D	CA	4.8
Gresham, Dolores	R	TN	4.8
McComas, Danny	R	NC	
Mooney, Alex	R	MD	
Ohrenschall, Genie	D	NV	
Prentice, Margarita	D	WA	4.7
Sawyer, Tom	D	KS	
Skinner, Mary	R	WA	
Vaughn, Gloria	R	NM	

year, and he was subsequently appointed to fill out the remainder of the dead man's term. In 1986, he was elected to the Kansas House and has been re-elected ever since. In 1998, Sawyer ran for Kansas governor but lost to Republican Governor Bill Graves (Ferguson 1998). He has faced only token opposition since first being elected to the Kansas House of Representatives. Sawyer's Wichita district is about 11 percent Latino and 6 percent African American, which makes it a majority-white district.

Representative Mary Skinner (R-WA) represents a majority-white district outside of the heart of liberal Seattle. Her district is 26 percent Latino and 1 percent African American. Senator Alex Mooney (R-MD) represents a majority-white district in Frederick, Maryland, with only a 12 percent African-American and Latino population. Like Skinner, Representative Danny McComas (R-NC) has been elected in a major-ity-white district with a substantial African-American population (34 percent) and only a 7 percent Latino population. McComas, however, sees his role as representing his constituents as "first and foremost" (Rice 2002). He aims to appeal to white conservative voters in his rural North Carolina district and thus emphasizes his social conservatism in campaign announcements.

Of course, having an Anglo name is not always an advantage. At the 2003 NALEO Conference in Phoenix, Arizona, New Mexico State Representative James G. Taylor, a Latino Democrat, told me of his efforts to inform his Latino constituents that he was indeed one of them, despite his Anglo name. His electoral success depended on this because his 12th District is 71 percent Latino. In an unusual twist, he asked me, "How is it that a Latino named Taylor can get elected in a majority Latino New Mexico district?"

Like Taylor, Senator Margarita Prentice (D-WA) has chosen to emphasize her first name, and not her husband's name, in her liberal Seattle
district. The district has a 50 percent African-American population and
an 11 percent Latino population, making it a majority-minority district.
In such a district, the ability to form a black-brown coalition necessitates
an appeal to ethnic and minority solidarity, so that her constituents can
relate to her life experience.

Representative Dario Frommer (D-CA) represents a district with a 29
percent Latino population and a 3 percent African-American population.
Like Senator Prentice, he emphasized his first name in 2000, when he
ran in an open seat contest against two other Democrats. He won the
primary with 43 percent of the vote. In the general election, he defeated
his Republican challenger by a 59–41 percent margin. His ability to reach
out to Latino voters in the Democratic primary enabled him to go on to
win in the general election in a reliably Democratic California district.

For candidates who are not obviously Latino, campaign strategies will
vary depending on district composition. Six of the eleven Latinos find it
advantageous to advertise the fact that they are Latino, especially given
the strong pluralities of Latinos in their districts. This is more often the
case with Democrats, although Gloria Vaughn (R-NM) also advertises
her Latina heritage, primarily because of New Mexico's unique cultural
history (see Chapter 3 for more on New Mexico's Legislature). However,
four of the eleven Latinos – all Republicans – do not emphasize their
Latino heritage, but instead run as "white" candidates in very conservative white districts.

Near-Latino Majority Districts

In several districts, the Latino population is so close to a Latino majority
that Latinos have less difficulty winning such races. In many cases, Latinos
win the Democratic primary based on strong support from the Latino
community, and in the general election, they face either no opposition or
weak Republican opponents. In these districts, which I define as those that
are between 45 and 49.9 percent Latino, African Americans combine with
Latinos to form majorities. In fact, the only two Latino members of the
U.S. House of Representatives from non-Latino majority districts come
from this type of district. As Table 4.6 shows, three state legislators fall
into this category, including one state senator, Bob Coffin (D-NV). All five
districts have combined Latino and African-American majorities.

U.S. Senator Bob Menéndez (D-NJ) has seen his political career rise in
unprecedented ways. As the highest-ranking Latino in the U.S. House and
Democratic Caucus Chair, Menéndez spoke to a primetime audience the

TABLE 4.6. *Latino Legislators in Near-Majority Districts (45 Percent and Up)*

Name	Party	State	Also in Table
Coffin, Bob	D	NV	4.7
Díaz, Manny	D	CA	4.7
*Menéndez, Bob	D	NJ	4.7
Oropeza, Jenny	D	CA	4.7
*Velázquez, Nydia	D	NY	4.7

Notes:
* Names with stars indicate a member of the U.S. House

opening night at the 2004 Democratic National Convention in Boston. His former district in Northern New Jersey has a 47 percent Latino population and a 13 percent African-American population. Born in Cuba, Menéndez previously served in the New Jersey State Senate before being elected to represent the newly created majority-minority 13th Congressional District in 1992. He began his political career by first being elected to the Union City school board in 1974. In 1987, he successfully ran for the New Jersey Legislature, where he served until his election to Congress. He easily won the 1992 Democratic primary with over two-thirds of the vote, and since his district is heavily Democrat, subsequently won the general election. As a Cuban American, Menéndez has been a strong supporter of the trade embargo on Cuba while at the same time advocating a progressive agenda on just about every other issue facing his district and later state. In 2003, House Democrats rewarded him by electing him the Democratic Caucus Chairman, making him the highest-ranking Latino ever in Congress.[7] When then-U.S.-Senator Jon Corzine (D-NJ) decided to run for governor after the resignation of James E. McGreevey, he appointed Menéndez to serve out the remainder of his term. In 2006, Menéndez ran for election against the son of former New Jersey Governor Thomas Kean and defeated him, becoming New Jersey's first elected Latino U.S. Senator.

Minority Coalitions

Minority coalitions can also help explain the election of Latinos to districts with non-Latino majorities. In districts with a combined majority of African Americans and Latinos, it is hardly a surprise when a member

[7] U.S. Representative Nydia Velázquez (D-NY) will be discussed in the next section under Minority Coalitions.

TABLE 4.7. *Latino Legislators in Districts with Combined Latino and African-American Majorities*

Name	Party	State	% Latino	% Black	Also in Table
Caraballo, Wilfredo	D	NJ	35	41	
Coffin, Bob	D	NV	45	9	4.6
Díaz, Manny	D	CA	47	4	4.6
Marín, Pedro	D	GA	30	25	
*Menéndez, Robert	D	NJ	47	13	4.6
Olivo, Dora	D	TX	32	34	
Oropeza, Jenny	D	CA	45	15	4.6
Pichardo, Juan	D	RI	5	5	
Pou, Nellie	D	NJ	39	23	
Prentice, Margarita	D	WA	11	50	4.5
Ramírez, Víctor	D	MD	23	60	
Ramos, Phil	D	NY	42	19	4.2
Reinoso, Felipe	D	CT	44	31	4.2
*Velázquez, Nydia	D	NY	49	13	4.6
Zamarripa, Sam	D	GA	8	62	4.8

Notes: Names with stars indicate a member of the U.S. House.

of one of the two groups is elected to office. In many instances, the party elite decides which candidate will get support, thus driving challengers away, at least until the seat opens. In fact, the two Latino members of Congress elected from non-Latino majority districts come from these types of districts (Representatives Nydia Velázquez, D-NY, and Albio Sires, D-NJ). Many of the African-American members of Congress have been elected from such districts, primarily because of the ability of the African-American political establishment to mobilize voters. Latinos still have lower participation rates and less of a cohesive group identity. As Table 4.7 shows, other than the two members of the U.S. House, thirteen Latino legislators nationwide represent districts that have combined Latino and African-American majorities, whereas fifty-two Latinos represent districts with white majorities. All thirteen legislators are Democrats from ten states around the country. Four of the thirteen legislators serve in the upper chambers (Georgia, Nevada, Rhode Island, and Washington).

Senator Juan Pichardo of Rhode Island is the highest-ranking Dominican-American elected official in the United States. Born in the Dominican Republic, he came to the United States when he was a young boy. He began his political career by first serving as a campaign manager for a local state representative and then running and winning a seat on the Democratic State Committee, in which he served for several years. In 2000, he ran for a State Senate seat against a white twelve-year incumbent and lost by ninety-six votes in the primary. Two years later, as a result of redistricting changes, he ran in his new district against African-American incumbent Senator Charles Walton and defeated him largely because the redistricting changes had reduced the number of African Americans in the district (from 26 to 21 percent) and increased the number of Latinos (from 41 to 47 percent).

As a majority-minority district, then, it is of little surprise that a Latino Democrat would win a seat, although this is an upper chamber seat in which an incumbent was defeated. In this district, however, given the choice between a Latino Democrat and an African-American Democrat, Latino voters opted for a Latino to represent them, as attested by the outcome. In a neighboring district, Latino Leon Tejada defeated an African-American incumbent for a seat in the State General Assembly in what became a majority-Latino district.

An African-American representative running in another nearby district noted, "every Latino who ran is light- or white-skinned. What we have in common is that we come in shades, and we need to accept that within ourselves, as who we are … we're more apt to run against ourselves than someone white" (Kurland 2001). He also surmised that Latinos feared taking on the power structure and instead chose to challenge liberal African-American incumbents with support from the white elite. This charge exposes the tension between the two communities in Providence. In my interview with Senator Pichardo (D-RI), he acknowledged that there were tensions between the black and Latino community, but he was determined to bridge those differences by focusing on issues that matter to both communities, such as predatory lending, consumer protection, and expanding economic opportunities for all of the people in his district.[8]

Prior to being elected to the Georgia State Senate, Sam Zamarripa was an investment banker and had amassed the funds needed to launch a successful bid for the State Senate. In the primary, he defeated Brenda Muhammad, an African-American woman involved in Atlanta's educational system, by a 53–47 percent margin after having come in second prior to the runoff (Charkaborty 2003). His district is 62 percent African American and only 7 percent Latino. Zamarripa still sees himself as a Latino leader yet focuses on issues such as poverty, health care, and racism

[8] Interview with Senator Pichardo, NHCSL Conference, 2006.

in his public statements – issues to which African-American voters can relate. Both Pichardo and Zamarripa defeated African-American candidates in Democratic primaries, which reflects some tension between the African-American and Latino community.

Representative Felipe Reinoso (D-CT) was first elected in 2000 by defeating Representative Héctor Díaz in the Democratic primary. He was then challenged by a Latino Democrat in the 2002 primary and beat him, receiving almost two-thirds of the vote. In the general election, he beat a Latino Republican by an even larger margin. His district is 44 percent Latino and 31 percent African American. Unlike Pichardo and Zamarripa's districts, however, Reinoso went on to challenge a Latino Republican, giving the African-American voters in his district an easy choice in line with their strong Democratic partisanship.

Representative Phil Ramos (D-NY) represents a district created following the 2000 Census as a majority-minority district in Suffolk County. Prior to running for his seat in 2002, Ramos served for twenty years as a member of the Suffolk County Police Department, rising to the level of detective when he retired. His district is 42 percent Latino and 19 percent African American. He defeated a Latino Republican, Phil Goglas, in the 2002 election by a comfortable margin in this heavily Democratic district. Like Reinoso, Ramos benefited in the general election from the strong support of African Americans who chose him over a Latino Republican. It would be interesting to have seen how an African-American Republican would have fared against either Reinoso or Ramos.

In some cases, Latino legislators have run unopposed in the Democratic primary because of strong party support. For example, Puerto Rican–born Representative Pedro Marín (D-GA) moved to Atlanta in 1995 and currently serves an urban district that is more diverse than Casas' district in that 30 percent of the population is Latino and 25 percent is African American, making it a majority-minority district. He ran unopposed in the 2002 primary and general election.

His ability to run unopposed is remarkable given the fact that no African Americans have challenged him in the primary in a district that has a 25 percent African-American population. In my interview with Marín, he indicated that he had worked in the community for seven years and was recruited by party leaders to run for this open seat in 2002. His theme of "building safer and stronger communities" is especially appealing given that the district is very small geographically, with 70 percent of its residents renting condominiums or apartments. Its population is mobile and transient, making it especially difficult to campaign. Marín says, "I was elected with support from blacks and senior citizens more so than Latinos. Even though the district is 30 percent Latino, the number of registered Latino voters is below 1,000."[9] The small white population, however, has not put up a candidate to challenge Marín, which is unexpected given that minorities have lower rates of voter participation, although it would be difficult to overcome a 55 percent minority population for a white Republican candidate in Atlanta.

U.S. Congresswoman Nydia Velázquez (D-NY) was born in Puerto Rico and moved to New York City in the early 1980s, following a teaching career at the University of Puerto Rico. She began her political career by running for the New York City Council in 1984, after gaining some political experience working for U.S. Representative Ed Towns (D-NY). Like Menéndez, she ran for Congress in 1992 in a newly created district carved out of then-U.S. Representative Stephen Solarz's (D-NY) old congressional district. Sensing the opportunity to win in a district with a 49 percent Latino population and a 9 percent African-American population, Velázquez challenged Solarz, a Jewish Democrat, and another liberal Latina Democrat, Elisabeth Colón. She received the endorsement of then-Mayor David Dinkins and Reverend Jesse Jackson and defeated Solarz by a 34–28 percent margin. She ultimately won the general election in a district that gave former Vice President Al Gore 77 percent of the vote in the 2000 presidential election. As the 1992 primary makes clear, her victory would not have been possible were it not for a biracial coalition between African Americans and Latinos.

Multicandidate Primaries

As alluded to earlier in the chapter, in many districts, Latinos have been successful winning non-Latino majority seats precisely because of their ability to win multicandidate (usually Democratic) primaries; I define multicandidate primaries as those in which a candidate has more than one opponent in a party primary. Multicandidate primaries provide Latino candidates an advantage because the threshold for winning is much lower in primaries. Candidates do not need a majority of votes to win – just a plurality. Additionally, it is easier for Latino candidates to mobilize a strong base of Latino voters in what usually turns out to be a low-turnout election populated by more than two candidates in many races. Of course, such strategies are complicated by the historically low Latino turnout in all kinds of elections. In these districts, the probability

---

[9] Interview with Representative Pedro Marín, NHCSL Conference, 2005.

TABLE 4.8. *Latino Legislators Who Initially Won in Multicandidate Primaries*

Name	Party	State	Number in Primary	Also in Table
Aguilera, John	D	IN	3	
Álvarez, Manny	D	AZ	3	
Barrientos, Gonzalo	D	TX	2	
Bustamante, Ernest	D	AZ	3	
Frommer, Dario	D	CA	3	4.5
García, Michael	D	CO	4	
Gresham, Dolores	R	TN	3	4.5
Gutiérrez, Ana Sol	D	MD	7	
Vas, Joseph	D	NJ	3	
Zamarripa, Sam	D	GA	3	4.7

of Republican candidates winning the general election is low, even if they are minorities. In a similar vein, there are some solidly Republican districts where the winner of its primary becomes the de facto winner in the general election. Note, however, that there is only one Latino Republican who was initially elected in a multicandidate primary.

As Table 4.8 shows, ten Latinos were first elected in multicandidate primaries. Two of the ten Latinos serve in the upper chamber.

Ernest Bustamante was first elected to the Arizona House in 2002. He first beat the incumbent, Mark Clark, by 900 votes in a three-way Democratic primary and then won the general election against Republican Brett Benedict in a district with a 30 percent Latino population and a 3 percent African-American population. The other incumbent, Democrat Cheryl Chase, was effectively re-elected to the other assembly seat from the 23rd District. Bustamante initially ran against Clark in 2000 in an eight-way Democratic primary and lost by only 92 votes amid controversy that the Clark family engaged in unscrupulous practices to ensure Clark's election.

John Aguilera hails from Western Indiana in a district that has a 22 percent Latino population and a 10 percent African-American population. Despite the fact that this district is not majority-Latino, Aguilera has been actively involved in the promotion of Latino issues, and he touts his identity on his website and in his legislative activities. His father was a union representative in the steel industry, which introduced him to political activity early in life. He began his political career by becoming the first Latino elected to the county council in 1994. He was initially elected to the state legislature in 2000, when he narrowly won by 200 votes against two other Democratic opponents in the primary, which clinched his victory because no Republican challenged him in the general election. Like nearby Chicago, machine politics is alive and well in Northern Indiana and exerts its influence during the Democratic primaries.[10] His district, although majority-white, is heavily Democratic. In 2002, he defeated the same opponent in the Democratic primary and had no Republican opponent in the general election.

Ana Sol Gutiérrez (D-MD) represents several suburbs of Washington, DC, where the vast majority of Latinos are Salvadoran, like herself. Although her district is 18 percent Latino and 13 percent African American, Montgomery County's white voters are progressive, with many of them federal government employees. She started her political career by running and serving on the Montgomery County Board of Education in 1990, where she served until 1998. That year, she ran for the House of Delegates and lost in the Democratic primary. In 2002, she ran again for the same seat and won in a crowded, seven-way Democratic primary, defeating twelve-year incumbent Delegate Leon Billings.[11]

Unlike Bustamante, Aguilera, and Gutiérrez, Dolores R. Gresham is a Latina Republican elected in conservative Tennessee. She was initially elected in 2002 when she ran against two other opponents. She is a retired Marine Corps lieutenant colonel who ran in an open seat contest and won a tough primary against white opponents in a district that has only a 2 percent Latino population and a 21 percent African-American population. Unlike the Democratic candidates, Gresham did not win the primary by appealing to Latinos since they are such a small percentage of the district, much less the Republican Party. She touts her conservative credentials, including her anti-gun control and anti-abortion beliefs. Additionally, she has assumed her husband's Anglo last name – hardly a liability in the rural South.

Gonzalo Barrientos (D-TX) represented culturally vibrant and diverse Austin in a district that has a 29 percent Latino population and an 11 percent African-American population. The white population, largely made up of intellectuals and bohemians, are much more liberal than the typical white Texan. Senator Barrientos has been active in Latino causes. He was one of César Chávez' organizers in central Texas during the Civil Rights Movement, and participates in events in the Austin Latino community. He is a staunch advocate of organized labor, education funding,

---

[10] Interview with Representative John Aguilera, NHCSL Conference, 2005.
[11] In Maryland, there are three seats per district in the House of Delegates. Like New Jersey, this may facilitate the ability of Latino candidates to win as part of a biracial coalition.

and civil rights. He was first elected to the Texas House in 1975, where he served until 1984. That year, he ran for the State Senate in a crowded Democratic primary to replace Lloyd Doggett, who is now the U.S. Representative from the Austin area. He has subsequently been re-elected every four years.[12]

Multicandidate primaries help level the playing field by enabling Latino candidates to win in non-Latino majority districts. A single political party dominates most districts in the United States, and the primary election is where we sometimes see competition. Because Latinos comprise a large percentage of the Democratic voters in many districts, Latinos have the ability to mobilize their base and win primaries in heavily Democratic districts, thus ensuring their election to the seat. This does not mean that Latinos nominated from such districts are necessarily radical or embody the "politics of difference," to use Canon's (1999a) terminology. Like the supply-side argument Canon makes in his book, Latinos elected in such districts ultimately must embody the politics of commonality to appeal to non-Latino voters in their districts. At the same time, however, we have not seen this pattern for Latino Republicans. Representative Gresham was elected in her conservative district *despite* her Latino background. That is, she neither appealed to nor owes her election to Latino voters, or the party establishment for that matter. Interestingly, only one of these districts (Zamarripa) has a combined African-American and Latino majority, indicating that for the most part, there is very little elite competition between Latinos and African Americans in such primaries.

Latino Republicans

Republican Latinos are much more likely to be elected from districts with smaller Latino (i.e., majority-white) populations. Democratic Latinos are more likely to get elected and serve in districts with high minority populations. Most Latino legislators are Democratic, and the few that are Republican generally represent districts with substantial numbers of white voters. This is certainly the case for Latinas, as well. In many cases, Latino Republicans choose not to advertise their Latino heritage and thus are not candidates of choice by most Latino voters. All Latina representatives with the exception of (former Senator) Olga Mendez from New York and the two New Mexico Latina Republicans

---

[12] In 2006, Senator Barrientos retired from the State Senate. He was replaced by Kirk Watson, the former mayor of Austin.

represent majority-white districts. This has several consequences. Many of these Latina Republicans do not advertise their Latina heritage, and in some cases are spouses of white husbands and opt to take their husband's name (as shown later for Representative Gresham). Mendez was first elected as a Democrat to her majority-Latino district in 1978 and later switched to the Republican Party in 2002 so that she could have more influence in the New York State Senate, controlled by Republicans since the 1960s. She subsequently lost a re-election race to the son of U.S. Representative Jose Serrano, D-NY, in 2004. She died of cancer in 2009, and in her *New York Times* obituary, Sewell Chan wrote that "Mrs. Mendez insisted on being known as Puerto Rican and rejected the terms Hispanic and Latino."

Representative Joseph Miro (R-New Castle, DE) represents a majority-white moderate Republican district in suburban Delaware. A Cuban American, Miro was elected President of the National Hispanic Caucus of State Legislators. His district is a typical Northeastern Republican district: fiscally conservative and socially liberal. His primary opponents are often white Republicans who are more socially conservative than he is. In his district, Asian Americans are the largest minority, and Astro Zeneca, MBNA, and the University of Delaware are the largest employers.

Representative Elvira Reyna (R-Mesquite, TX) represents a majority-white district in the Dallas suburbs with a 17 percent Latino population and a 14 percent African-American population.[13] She was first elected to the Texas House in 1993 after Bill Blackwood, for whom she worked, died while serving his term. Friends and colleagues encouraged her to run for the seat given her experience working for the representative. She did run and won a special election and has been re-elected unopposed since 1996, with the exception of 2000, when Democrat Bruce Archer challenged her and lost by a 58–42 percent margin.

California's only Latina Republican legislator, Bonnie Garcia, was elected in 2002 from Riverside County. She was actively involved in Governor Arnold Schwarzenegger's campaign for governor and has received his support in her campaign. She was born in New York and touts her "mainstream" credentials in a district with a 60 percent Latino majority. Because of her district demographics, Garcia touts her commitment to the Latino community, despite her non-Mexican-American background. Latino Republicans, then, adjust their campaign tactics

---

[13] Representative Reyna was defeated in a Republican primary in 2006.

according to the demographics of the district. If their districts have substantial Latino populations, they are more likely to tout their Latino identity and let voters know that they are genuinely interested in the issues that affect the community.

Conclusion

Latinos are becoming contenders in districts that are not majority-Latino. Even though only two Latinos have been elected to the U.S. House from districts that are not majority-Latino, it is only a matter of time before more Latinos are elected to legislative seats in non-Latino majority districts or states. In 2004, Colorado Attorney General Ken Salazar (D) won an open U.S. Senate seat left vacant by Sen. Ben Nighthorse Campbell (R-CO), the only Native American in the Senate. In Florida, Mel Martínez won the open U.S. Senate seat left vacant by Sen. Bob Graham (D). Now that both major political parties see Latino votes as crucial in their electoral success, we will undoubtedly see more Latino elected officials serving non-Latino majority districts and states.

Initially, Latino legislators who won in non-Latino majority districts were aided by elite-driven policies aimed at increasing minority representation. Much in the same way African Americans gained legislative seats, early Latino elected officials began their careers in legislatures representing heavily Latino districts. Additionally, as in the case of five Latino legislators, party elites, such as the state governor, have appointed Latinos to serve in non-Latino majority districts. There are a couple of reasons why a governor would want to do this. First, she may want to increase her standing among the state's Latino voters in her bid for re-election, especially if she is a Republican candidate in a politically competitive state. Second, she may see an opportunity to appoint a talented Latino to give him a boost in his electoral career.

The Republican Party especially has made an active effort to recruit and financially support Latino Republicans interested in running for political office, often in majority-white districts. Five Latinos out of the sixty-five nationwide were clearly recruited by the party leaders to run in safe Republican districts in mostly Midwestern and Southern states. This activity runs parallel to Republican Party efforts in presidential campaigns to appeal to moderate white voters, especially suburban women, who may be more inclined to vote for Republican candidates who are more tolerant (Fraga and Leal 2004). Moreover, fifty-two of the sixty-five

Latinos represent majority-white districts, and the Republican Latinos come from these districts. No Republican is elected from a majority-minority district (see Table 4.7). Such elite-driven practices have helped Latino legislators grow in number.

As Table 4.7 shows, however, several Latinos began to get elected in districts with combined African-American and Latino majorities, thus benefiting from biracial coalitions. Politicians of all ethnicities take advantage of the electoral system and its accompanying rules to try to increase their probability of winning. Latino legislators who live in districts with strong Latino pluralities and African-American populations have mobilized their base while at the same time appealing to African Americans in order to win the de facto election in many districts – namely the Democratic primary. As Browning, Marshall, and Tabb (1984) demonstrate in the urban setting, Latinos have in many cases benefited from biracial coalitions. On the other hand, in some locales, Latino and African-American elites have sparred over the ability of some Latinos, like Senators Juan Pichardo (D-RI) and Sam Zamarripa (D-GA), to defeat African-American incumbents.

Eleven of the sixty-five Latinos serving in non-Latino majority districts have names that are not obviously Latino. In these cases, Democrats and Republicans have been elected in states ranging from North Carolina to Washington. Seven of the eleven are Latinas who have married non-Latinos and have chosen to take their husbands' names. There are probably a couple of reasons for this. The simplest explanation is that these women have not consciously chosen to suppress their Latino identity but nonetheless have chosen to take their husbands' names. Some, however, may choose to disguise their Latino identity to increase their probability of winning, although this would be difficult to test empirically (Cartagena 2004). Either way, as Latinos become more assimilated and intermarry with whites, this trend is likely to continue in future elections. In fact, Census 2000 data indicate that foreign-born Asians and foreign-born Hispanics have higher rates of intermarriage than do U.S.-born whites and blacks. Additionally, approximately one-third of third-generation Latinas are married to non-Latinos.

Because many Latinos self-identify as "white," and because growing assimilation will probably change white attitudes about who is included in this category, we will likely see more Latinos elected to white-majority districts in the near future. African Americans will still face difficulties precisely because of the long legacy of discrimination and the ever-permanent racial divide (Dawson 1994). As Latinos become part of the American mainstream and intermarry with whites, more Latinos will be elected to state legislative seats as well as congressional seats. Through elite-driven methods, features of the electoral system, and Latinos with non-Latino names, the growing number of Latinos serving in state legislatures and Congress can be better understood.

5

Voices from Within

How Latino Legislators See Themselves

"I don't carry a shield that says 'I am a Democrat' or 'I'm a Latina'. I represent my district."

– Rep. Fran Coleman (D-Denver)

Pennsylvania State Representative Angel Cruz (D-Philadelphia), a Puerto Rican who represents a majority-Latino district, recounted a story about one of his constituents – a little girl named Delimar Vera who was presumed dead after being kidnapped from her home when she was a newborn. The kidnapper subsequently set fire to the home so that the Fire Department would think that the newborn had perished in the fire. Delimar's mother never believed her daughter had perished in the fire, but because of her difficulty communicating in English, she was never able to pursue the matter any further. Then, one day six years later, Delimar's mother attended a birthday party for a friend and noticed a young girl who resembled herself and her other children. She now had a Latino representative and decided to contact him and recount her story in Spanish. She enlisted the help of Representative Cruz, who helped her pursue DNA tests and file the appropriate police reports. At the end of the day, Representative Cruz was able to reunite Delimar with her mother.

The above story illustrates the extent to which Representative Cruz saw himself as a public servant. Delimar's mother contacted Cruz presumably because she trusted him and could speak to him in *her* language. Cruz indicated to me that he felt a responsibility to help Latinos in Philadelphia, even if he did not represent them because he is the *only* Latino in the Pennsylvania Legislature.

Kansas Representative Mario Goico (R-Wichita) represents a district that is only 1 percent Latino. Why would it be in his interest, one might ask, to attend a conference of Hispanic State Legislators? His district is barely Latino, and the issues his district cares about cannot be the same as someone who represents a majority-Latino district. Goico is not a professional politician. He has an engineering degree and worked for many years as an airline pilot. He came to the United States alone as a teenager from Cuba as part of Operation Pedro Pan. He was placed with a host family in Wichita, Kansas, and remained there ever since. He became involved in the Chamber of Commerce and eventually ran for state representative, winning in a largely white Republican district. In the legislature, Goico described how he helped defeat a bill that would have barred noncitizens from receiving in-state tuition in Kansas colleges and universities. As he told me, "if I wouldn't have been there, it would have passed" the committee and the floor.[1]

New Mexico Senator Carlos Cisneros (D-Taos) comes from a family that has been in modern-day New Mexico since the Spanish colonial period. Senator Cisneros began his political career as a county commissioner and president of the local union. He has worked for the oil and gas industry for over twenty years. His district is majority-Latino, as are many others in New Mexico. The number-one issue in his district is not immigration or even education, but water rights. His district includes many Pueblos, which are sovereign nations of Native Americans. Conservation and environmental stewardship are important issues in New Mexico. Like many other New Mexicans present, Cisneros was proud of his governor, Bill Richardson, who is the only Latino governor in the United States. Coming from a state that is over 40 percent Latino, Cisneros undoubtedly has had a different experience than someone representing a district with hardly any Latinos at all.

As the earlier profiles indicate, Latino legislators are a diverse group of individuals that come from all parts of the country. Whether it is Spanish American Michel Consejo (D-Vermont), who represents a district with less than 100 Latinos, or Mexican American Ryan Guillen (D-Texas), who represents a district in the Rio Grande Valley with an overwhelming majority of Latinos, we see a common bond that unites Latino legislators (more on this later in the chapter). Even though Consejo's constituents care about different issues than Guillen's constituents, this does not mean that these two individuals have nothing in common. As I show further

---

[1] Personal interview, November 18, 2006. What is important is Goico's *belief* that he made a difference. Whether he *actually* caused the death of this bill is unknown.

in the chapter, a Latino identity exists among legislators, which arguably does not exist among the rank and file, but it is something that is
cultivated and encouraged by the existence of pan-ethnic organizations,
such as the National Hispanic Caucus of State Legislators (NHCSL).
As Schmidt et al. (2000) observe, "recognition of cultural similarities
generates a sense of 'we-ness' that leads many, although not all, Latina/os
to feel an affinity across national origin, generational, class, gender, and
sexuality differences ..." This is certainly borne out by Latino state legislators, who represent the diversity of the Latino community. Of course,
those who do not perceive or desire a Latino pan-ethnic identity simply
do not participate in such gatherings.

How do Latino legislators see themselves? How do Latino legislators
perceive their districts? Do Latino legislators sense particular challenges
in terms of electoral success and policy-making success? Do Latino legislators overwhelmingly concern themselves with "Latino" issues? What is
the extent of partisanship vis-à-vis ethnicity? This chapter addresses all
of these questions by examining data gathered from a series of interviews
with Latino legislators from all parts of the country, as well as archival data culled from various sources. This chapter suggests the growing
mainstreaming of Latinos in American society in that Latino legislators expressed concerns regarding issues that are not traditionally seen
as "Latino issues." At the same time, the interviews suggest that Latino
legislators share a sense of linked fate.

Most of the work on Latino representation has examined roll call
votes as indicative of the extent to which Latinos are substantively represented. To date, however, little if any work has examined how Latino
legislators view themselves (Tien 2009). Whereas we know that legislators
are attuned to the needs of their districts (e.g., Mayhew 1974), we know
very little about the extent to which Latino legislators view themselves
as collective representatives of the entire Latino community. Previous
research has shown that African Americans and Latinos are more likely
to trust and contact coethnic legislators (Gay 2001; Pantoja and Segura
2003), yet we know very little about the effect this has on legislators and
their responsibility to their community, although see Minta (2009) for
research detailing the extent to which Latino representatives invest time
in advocating for their communities in committees.

Methodology

This section explains the methods used in the remainder of this chapter. It also explains in detail the questionnaire used to interview Latino

legislators. I conclude with some reflections as to why this approach is crucial for the understanding of how Latino legislators see their roles, and outline how future research projects could test many of the hypotheses more systematically.

The National Association of Latino Elected and Appointed Officials (NALEO) and the NHCSL hold annual conferences in June and November, respectively. For the past several years, I have attended these conferences to observe and interview Latino members of Congress and state legislators. In total, twenty-three Latino legislators were interviewed from a variety of districts (see Table 5.1 for demographics). I conducted interviews during breaks, and they typically lasted approximately fifteen minutes each. I used a "snowball" method of interviewing legislators. In one instance, the president of the organization assisted me by making other legislators at the conference aware of my presence. Many of the quotes and narratives of this chapter come from several years of intensive immersion in these conferences, as well as discussions, both formal and informal, with Latino legislators.

The questionnaire I used is presented in the Appendix and is divided into several categories, each highlighting a specific nature of how Latino legislators view themselves. The first set of questions are aimed at discovering the political past and backgrounds of Latino legislators. Are Latinos like other politicians in terms of how they become interested in politics? Do political trajectories differ among Latino candidates, and if so, how? Then a series of questions are asked about the election to the current position, including how they perceive the competitiveness of their districts and the nature of primary and general election opponents. I also ask about the nature of the current district, inviting legislators to tell a bit more about the district they represent. This open-ended approach allows for a window into how the legislator perceives her constituency, just as Fenno (1978) did in his seminal work. Fowler and McClure (1990) have studied political ambition more broadly, but the next set of questions I asked were aimed at understanding the considerations that *Latinos* weigh when deciding whether to run for higher offices. As the women and politics literature demonstrates, gender differences also emerge, as discussed later in the chapter.[2]

---

[2] A note about selection bias: I am well aware that not all Latino legislators attend such meetings, but given the partisan, gender, subethnic, and regional diversity I encountered in my interviews, as well as attendance at more than just one conference, I think my approach will yield valuable insights into the nature of Latino representation in state legislatures. Such insights cannot be gleaned from a mail survey that, as one legislator I interviewed told me, "I never respond to."

Background, Political Past, and Election to Current Position

In terms of political background, every legislator has a different story, although a surprising number of Latino legislators began their political careers through the labor movement. This is a different path than for most African Americans, who cultivate their political skills in the black church (Harris 1999; McDaniel 2008; Verba, Scholzman, and Brady 1995). None of the legislators I interviewed indicated the church as their conduit to political life. The background and political past of all the Latino legislators interviewed can be classified in three ways: volunteer, union, or personal/issue-based.

Eleven Latino legislators indicated that they first became involved in politics by volunteering for other candidates. Many legislators volunteered for other candidates because their parents were involved in politics, either in their home countries or in the United States. Georgia Representative Pedro Marín notes, "When I grew up in Puerto Rico, my father was involved in politics. He organized caravans and petitions on the island. In 1984, I helped a candidate in Puerto Rico as his campaign manager, and then when I moved to Georgia because of my job, I decided to get involved in politics."[3] Another avenue of involvement in politics is from the family. Texas Senator Leticia van de Putte became involved in politics when her godfather ran for the state legislature. She campaigned on his behalf, was able to see what a campaign was like, and then ultimately decided to run for the State House in 1990. Connecticut Representative David Aldarondo volunteered for campaigns when he was not teaching in his high school classroom. He then decided to challenge an incumbent for state representative and was ultimately successful, largely, he claims, because of the contacts he made during his volunteer efforts. These are but a few illustrations of the myriad of ways that volunteering for another candidate can be an effective way to enter into the political process.

The labor movement has also had a crucial impact on the political lives of Latino legislators. Four Latino legislators I interviewed indicated that they became involved in politics through union activity. Some, like New Mexico Senator Carlos Cisneros, rose to become president of their local union and used that political accomplishment to run for political office. Others, like New Mexico Senator James Taylor, learned political skills from his union electrician father, who "always had a campaign sign in

[3] Personal Interview, November 2005.

his yard." Taylor started campaigning for candidates when he was twelve years old. In the Bronx, New York, Senator Efraín González, began union organizing as a child. When he was nineteen years old, he became the Transport Workers Union Chief. He was on the negotiating committee and was able to meet important political leaders in his role. He used these political skills to run for Democratic district leader and ultimately for the State Senate. As might be expected, no Latino Republicans indicated the labor movement in their political backgrounds.

Yet other legislators become involved in politics because of a certain issue or personal idiosyncratic reasons. Just as Representative Carolyn McCarthy (D-NY) ran for Congress after a deranged gunman killed her husband on the Long Island Railroad, many Latino legislators became involved in politics because they perceived ineffective or unresponsive government. Colorado Representative Rafael Gallegos worked for the federal government for thirty-eight years and was prohibited under the Hatch Act from getting involved in political races. When he retired, he finally seized the opportunity to run for office. Connecticut Representative Minnie González was a mother of three, on welfare, and struggling to make ends meet. She volunteered for other candidates and at phone banks when her youngest daughter was ten years old. She ultimately ran for state representative in order to be a voice for those who, like her several years ago, struggle through life's challenges. Rhode Island Representative Grace Díaz worked in home child care and had no previous involvement in politics, either in her home country of the Dominican Republic or in Providence. When then-Rhode Island Governor Don Carcieri imposed additional burdens and regulations on home child care providers, Díaz organized against his plans and eventually was asked to run for state representative by her supporters.

Most often, a legislator is not elected to the state legislature on the first try, nor is it the first office she runs for. Most of the legislators I interviewed ran for some other office prior to becoming a state legislator. This is the pattern most in line with previous research on political trajectories (Fowler and McClure 1990). The majority of the legislators I interviewed (sixteen out of twenty-five), however, first became legislators not by defeating an incumbent but by winning an open seat election. The few who did defeat incumbents strategically ran against vulnerable legislators who had, for example, "done a terrible job" in the case of Michel Consejo's (D-Vermont) Republican opponent.[4] In one case, Rhode Island

---

[4] Personal Interview, November 2007.

Senator Juan Pichardo defeated a twelve-year African-American incumbent in the Democratic primary by ninety-six votes. He decided to run against the incumbent primarily because the Providence district had become majority-Latino and that it was "inevitable that a Latino would eventually serve the district, so why not run?"

Legislators' Perceptions of Competitiveness

It is often assumed that legislators perceive their district to be much more competitive than it actually is. This is largely because of electoral uncertainty and the potential preferences of voters who may emerge to vote should the incumbent upset them (Arnold 1990). In my interviews, this was certainly the case, although few legislators exaggerated the perceived competitiveness of their districts. Although most districts are not electorally competitive, most indicated that the real contest, if at all, takes place in the primary. Legislators are also very good at remembering the precise margins of victory in their previous races. Legislators either reported that their districts were not competitive, competitive in the primary, or competitive in the general election.

In nine districts, legislators reported that they receive no serious challenges in the primary and/or general election, and are in safe districts. Kansas Representative Mario Goico reports that he runs unopposed in both the primary and general election in his conservative Wichita district. New Mexico Senator Carlos Cisneros reports that he draws no serious challengers either in the primary or in general election in his 87 percent Democratic district in Los Alamos. Massachusetts Representative Jeffrey Sánchez's district is so overwhelmingly Democratic that he estimates there are more independents than Republicans in his district. Since his initial victory, he has run unopposed. It is not necessarily the case that the only "safe" districts are majority-Latino, because Goico and Sánchez represent majority-white districts, one heavily Democratic and one heavily Republican.

In most heavily Democratic or heavily Republican districts, the de facto competition occurs in the party primary. Because of gerrymandering and redistricting aimed at protecting incumbents and political parties, districts have increasingly become more homogenous. This is certainly the case with many Latino legislators who reported somewhat difficult primaries but token opposition in the general election. For example, Connecticut Representative Minnie González indicated that she was challenged by Ilia Castro, a Latina "who was supported by the white political establishment." González claims she was outspent 15 to 1 in the primary and narrowly defeated her opponent, but the general election "was a blowout." "I always draw serious challenges in the primary," González remarked.[5] Fellow Connecticut Representative Juan Candelaria indicates that he "always has formidable Latino opponents in the primary… The policy differences are minimal – they are just people who want my seat."[6]

The situation is somewhat different for Latino Republicans. Delaware Representative Joe Miró notes that his major opposition is always in the primary, although his opponents are usually "white Republicans who are pro-life and more socially conservative than I am."[7] Michigan Senator Valde García was first elected in a seven-way Republican primary. He was the only Latino in a district with only a 3 percent Latino population. García indicates that he must fend off white libertarian candidates in the primary and, to a lesser extent, in the general election.

Even fewer districts are competitive in the general election. So-called "swing" districts have become rarer in recent decades (Oppenheimer 2005). This is no doubt true in the subset of Latino legislators I interviewed. Utah Representative Mark Archuleta Wheatley describes his district as competitive in the general election, remarking, "It's Utah after all." For a Democrat in Utah, he explains, "every election is competitive."[8] He won his 2004 race with 51 percent of the vote. New Mexico Senator James Taylor describes his district as a "swing" district, with a 58 percent registered Democratic advantage, although those are mostly conservative Democrats who vote for Republican presidential candidates. Taylor fends off his conservative Republican challengers by describing himself as a "New Mexico Democrat – pro-life and pro-gun."[9] Although he often attracts Green challengers because of some of his conservative positions, he nonetheless sees himself as representing his constituents well.

How They View Their Districts

Richard Fenno famously introduced the concept of concentric circles to describe how members of Congress viewed their districts. A constituency is not merely a constituency, as Fenno reminds us. Each member of

---

[5] Personal Interview, November 2006.
[6] Personal Interview, November 2006.
[7] Personal Interview, November 2005.
[8] Personal Interview, November 2005.
[9] Personal Interview, November 2007.

Congress perceives his district differently and in various layers (Fenno 1978). The question regarding Latino legislators is to what extent they see themselves as representatives of Latinos not only in their districts, but also in their state or nation. Do they see their districts first in partisan terms or by ethnic background? Do they see their districts in economic class terms, like working class? Do they see their districts first as rural or urban? Legislators described their districts in three major different ways: in partisan terms, in class terms, and in urban/rural terms.

When asked an open-ended question about the district they represent, nine Latino legislators first mentioned the partisan makeup of the district. New Mexico Senator Carlos Cisneros immediately mentioned the precise percentage of Democrats in his district (87 percent). Delaware Representative Joe Miró described his district as "heavily Republican, although not heavily conservative."[10] In the case of Cisneros, his district is majority-Latino, while Miró's district is majority-white. Rhode Island Representative Grace Díaz describes her district as "heavily Democratic and Dominican."[11] She also describes her experience in the legislature in partisan terms. Although Rhode Island is a heavily Democratic state, Republican Governor Donald Carcieri has been in office for several years, and she sees him and her Republican colleagues in the Legislature as pushing for anti-immigrant legislation. Indiana Representative John Aguilera, who represents Lake County in Northwest Indiana, describes his district as "strongly Democratic and machine politics driven, just like Chicago politics nearby."[12] Although all of these legislators are Latino and represent diverse districts, they still belong to one of two political parties, which forms part of their political identities.

More often than usual, the term "working class" emerged from legislators when asked to describe their districts. Overall, six legislators used class terms to describe their districts, mostly describing their constituents as working class, although Kansas Representative Mario Goico describes his district as "upper middle class and wealthy."[13] Texas Senator Leticia van de Putte describes her San Antonio district as "working class downtown San Antonio and the surrounding neighborhoods."[14]Arizona Senator Jorge García sees his district in much more explicit class terms than any of the other legislators: "My district is 10 percent wealthy,

[10] Personal Interview, November 2005.
[11] Personal Interview, November 2007.
[12] Personal Interview, November 2005.
[13] Personal Interview, November 2006.
[14] Personal Interview, November 2005.

and the rest poor, with working class neighborhoods in Tucson and the suburbs."[15]

The urban/rural divide is still strong in American politics, as attested by recent elections. Issues in rural areas are often different from issues in urban areas, and the wide diversity of Latino legislators represents this dichotomy. Georgia Representative Pedro Marín describes his district as "3 ½ mi long X 3 ½ mile wide in which 70 percent of his constituents are renters."[16] Because his district is so geographically small, the issues he cares about are distinct from large rural districts (more on this later). Like Marín's district, New York Representative Felix Ortíz' Brooklyn district is an urban multiethnic district composed of people from all over the world. On the other hand, some Southwestern districts are much different. Colorado Representative Rafael Gallegos's district covers an eight-county area in rural Colorado and includes many Latinos who live on farms, such as Interior Secretary Ken Salazar. New Mexico Representative Héctor Balderas's district is the second largest geographically in the state and includes many rural areas, along with Native American reservations. Vermont Representative Michel Consejo's district in a farming, rural part of the state near the Canadian border leads him to advocate for such policies as wider access to broadband internet. Latino legislators, therefore, do not solely come from heavily urbanized areas, although many do. Latino legislators who represent rural areas often bring their own set of issues to the Legislature, as we will see later in the chapter.

Issue Priorities of Latino Legislators

Like all legislators, Latino legislators are interested in representing their constituents well so as to continue to win re-election (Arnold 1990; Mayhew 1974). They will also organize their activities to make their goals of re-election easier. As such, legislators will do all they can to try to attract businesses and investment to their districts so that the economy is robust and unemployment is low. In my interviews, therefore, economic issues emerged as the most important for legislators, including budget decisions. Harold Lasswell once described politics as "who gets what, when, and how," and legislators constantly maneuver to procure as much as possible for their constituents. This is no different for Latino legislators. However, among the legislators I interviewed, other issues, endemic

[15] Personal Interview, November 2007.
[16] Personal Interview, November 2005.

to lower income communities, emerged as important. Education, health issues, public safety issues, and economic issues emerged – in the order of least cited to most cited importance – as the most pressing issues facing Latino legislators. Notably absent is immigration, which is perceived by many Americans as a salient issue for Latino voters. Because immigration is traditionally a federal issue, perhaps state legislators do not cite this issue with the same frequency as education, a traditional reserved power.

When asked in surveys, Latinos have consistently ranked education as the number-one issue affecting them. We should expect, then, that Latino legislators should report spending quite a bit of time working on the issue, whether on the floor, in committees, or in the community. Although many probably do, only three legislators *reported* it as the number-one issue. Four more reported education as the issue with which they spent the second-largest amount of time. New Mexico Senator James Taylor described education as one of his most important concerns; however, he sees the issue beyond ethnic terms: "Hispanic issues are mainstream issues. The Hispanic dropout rate in New Mexico is horrendous, but so is the dropout rate among rural whites in other states. We need to fix the problem so that all Americans benefit."[17] By heavily focusing on Latino issues, however, a white backlash might ensue. For example, Michigan Senator Valde García, a Republican, indicated that a white constituent was at first ambivalent about supporting his candidacy because of what he perceived as a possible immersion in "Latino" issues and thereby ignoring the concerns of his majority-white district. Afterward, the constituent told him: "I am glad you didn't do what I thought you would do and only focus on Hispanic issues."[18]

Texas Senator Leticia van de Putte described her number-one issue as education, largely because of the threat she sees from Republicans in the Texas Legislature, who "do nothing but cut programs" aimed at better educational opportunities.[19] Whereas Taylor and van de Putte are Democrats, Republicans such as Kansas Representative Mario Goico also described education as a key concern.

Three legislators cited health care issues as the most time consuming during their last legislative sessions. Two more cited health care issues as their second-most time consuming in their last legislative sessions.

[17] Personal Interview, November 2007.
[18] Personal Interview, November 2007.
[19] Personal Interview, November 2005.

In particular, the diabetes and obesity rates in the Latino community have increased markedly, and some legislators are attempting to address these concerns. In addition, some districts have high proportions of veterans. As most recently exemplified by the poor conditions of Walter Reed Hospital in Washington, DC, Texas Senator Leticia van de Putte places a particular emphasis on Veteran Affairs (VA) health care issues in her San Antonio district, which includes the Lackland Air Force Base and a correspondingly high number of veterans and retirees. New York Representative Felix Ortíz also describes health care as one of his most emphasized issues affecting his Brooklyn district.

Many Latino legislators described public safety issues as particularly important, largely because of the urban districts many represent. In particular, issues regarding crime, guns, drugs, gangs, and graffiti all emerged as concerns among some Latino legislators. For example, Georgia Representative Pedro Marín touted his efforts to pass an anti-graffiti bill in his urban Atlanta district: "I was the first Latino legislator in Georgia's history to have a bill become law. My graffiti bill requires that inmates clean graffiti on city streets, and also increased penalties for school trespassing in order to crack down on gang activities in our schools."[20] New Mexico Representative Héctor Balderas took on sex offenders in his short stint as a state representative. He sponsored HB 165, a law signed into law by Governor Bill Richardson, which required convicted sex offenders to register with law enforcement officials for life instead of the twenty years under then-New Mexico law. He later campaigned for the statewide office of State Auditor and was elected in 2006 at the age of 33, the youngest Latino elected statewide in New Mexico history.

By far the most legislators described the budget or other economic issues as requiring most of their time during the previous legislative sessions. This is to be expected given the importance of ensuring that each member procures enough funding to help her constituents for the ultimate goal of attaining re-election (Mayhew 1974). Ten legislators described such issues as consuming most of their time. Nine more described such issues as their second-most time-consuming activity. For example, Colorado Rep. Rafael Gallegos notes, "I want to be there for my constituents and develop economic growth to improve my people's economic well-being."[21] He added that the 2001 recession particularly affected his rural Colorado district. On the other hand, fiscally conservative Kansas Representative

[20] Personal Interview, November 2005.
[21] Personal Interview, November 2005.

Mario Goico spends most of his time promoting economic development in his district, including assisting small businesses and tax incentives to spur economic growth. New York Senator Efraín González reflected on his long career by describing his work on budgetary matters:

> I worked with Assembly colleagues and Sen. [Joseph] Bruno [Republican Majority Leader] for compromise and getting things done rather than getting credit. I also worked with [former U.S. Sen. Alfonse] D'Amato to bring home benefits to my constituents, despite the flack I got from my fellow Democrats.[22]

Senator González described the difficulty of being in the minority in the New York State Senate, which has been in Republican hands for several decades. His style of governance emphasized compromise and bipartisanship to deliver the goods for his poor district in the Bronx. Sometimes, being in leadership positions also requires additional attention to budgetary issues. This is the case for Arizona Senator Jorge García, the Assistant Democratic Leader, who described the budget as consuming nearly all of his time in his last legislative session.

Perceptions of Representation

Do Latino legislators view themselves distinctively? That is, how important is it to *them* that they are Latino in terms of the quality of representation for their Latino constituents? Much of the research surrounding this question involves the extent to which Latino or African-American *constituents* care that coethnics represent them (Gay 2001; Pantoja and Segura 2003). Few have asked, however, the extent to which Latino or African-American legislators perceive descriptive representation as important for the quality of responsiveness.

Six Latino legislators indicated that white or African-American legislators could represent their Latino constituents the same way as they could.[23] Often they pointed to examples of colleagues who they felt do a good job of representing their constituents of a different race or ethnicity. At the same time, however, many issued caveats about their answer, describing how difficult it would be for quality representation to occur. A

---

[22] Personal Interview, November 2007.
[23] This wording is admittedly vague – I let legislators interpret the question the way they wanted, so I could determine what *they* felt would be some of the similarities and differences, instead of imposing a predetermined narrative. In addition, it may have been the case that this was a politically tenable question, and/or respondents did not want to be thought of as racist if they expressed a superior ability to represent Latino constituents.

not insignificant number of Latino legislators also refused to answer the question, indicating that they do not know if non-Latino legislators could represent their constituents the same way as they could.

Massachusetts Representative Jeffrey Sánchez noted, "They all do. The real question is could they vs. do they? Do they understand the perspective of Latinos? African Americans would probably be better than whites for representing Latino interests."[24] For Sánchez, then, being a minority gives a legislator an added understanding of the particular issues that afflict underprivileged communities. Connecticut Representative David Aldarondo described that "race does not matter. It is best to look out for the interests of the community and be for the district."[25] Aldarondo pointed out that some of the most stalwart advocates of Latino immigrants were non-Latino, including Representative William Tong from Stamford, who he described as a passionate defender of Latino immigrants in the Connecticut General Assembly. Texas Senator Leticia van de Putte pointed out (now former) San Antonio Mayor Phil Hardberger as an example of someone who represents Latinos well even though he is Anglo, although she warns that it "does help to be Latino in order to understand the issues facing the community."[26] Among the Latino legislators indicating that non-Latinos could represent their Latino constituents well, most noted that it is more difficult for them to do so given their starting point, but that, in the end, it is possible.

Overall, however, Latino legislators were more likely to indicate that non-Latino legislators would not represent Latino constituents as effectively. Many cited a familiarity with the Latino community, including the ability to speak Spanish as the central reason for this. Representation, many argued, is more than just roll call voting. It involves standing up for the community and being there for their constituents. For those in states with low levels of Latino descriptive representation, the rationale becomes even stronger: Indiana Representative John Aguilera explains, "I am the only Latino legislator in Indiana, so I have a voice that can represent Latinos all over the state. If I am not there, who will represent us?"[27] This quote exemplifies the concept of *collective* representation, as opposed to dyadic representation (Weissberg 1978).[28] Even though

---

[24] Personal Interview, November 2007.
[25] Personal Interview, November 2005.
[26] Personal Interview, November 2005.
[27] Personal Interview, November 2005.
[28] Dyadic representation involves the direct representation between constituent and representative. Collective representation involves the representation of all

Aguilera has a district with constituents of all backgrounds, he feels an additional responsibility to represent Latinos from all parts of the state.

At the same time, however, being a Latino is not enough, according to some legislators. For New Mexico Senator Bernadette Sánchez, cultural and regional understanding is crucial: "It would be difficult for Latinos who have not spent a lot of time in New Mexico to represent Latino New Mexicans."[29] For New Mexico Senator James Taylor, being a native New Mexican and an educator is just as important as being Latino when it comes to representing Latinos. As we will see shortly, partisanship plays an important role in attitudes about descriptive representation.

A Latino in a position of power can also be empowering for Latinos. Bobo and Gilliam (1990) have argued that African Americans in positions of power can feel empowered when coethnics begin to run and win elections. In the same way, some Latino legislators feel that empowerment is an important benefit of descriptive representation. New York Senator Efraín González argues: "whites may be sympathetic to Latino interests, but I and other Latinos are more sensitive to Latino needs. I feel that Latino voters benefit from a sense of empowerment when they see Latinos in prestigious positions. Unity is strength." [30]As one of the founders of the NHCSL, González sees himself as a bridge builder. One of the reasons he started the organization was to create a network of legislators who could present a unified voice not only in their home states but also to corporate America regarding the issues that face Latinos, including the underrepresentation of Latinos on corporate boards and in positions of influence.

Does Partisanship Trump Ethnicity?

In recent decades, American politics has become more polarized, with conservatives opting into the Republican Party and progressives opting into the Democratic Party. The days of conservative Democrats and progressive Republicans are numbered, if not gone. This polarization has also filtered into Congress and state legislatures, where in most states, partisanship remains pronounced (Theriault 2009). Latino legislators, like all other legislators, often identify with a particular party, usually the Democratic Party. To assess the extent to which partisanship affects

---

members of the minority group by a representative even when they do not reside in the representative's district.

[29] Personal Interview, November 2006.

[30] Personal Interview, November 2007.

opinions about descriptive representation, legislators were asked whether a Latino (Republican or Democrat – opposite of them) would represent their Latino constituents the same way they do. This question was aimed at assessing the extent to which party mattered to them. By far the most of the legislators argued that a Latino of the opposite party could not represent their Latino constituents the same way, with various reasons provided. Some legislators, however, said that it was possible, albeit difficult because of the other party's many shortcomings.

Of those who argued that Latinos of the opposite party could represent Latino constituents well, many appealed to ideological and cultural explanations to describe their positions. For example, Arizona Senator Jorge García told me that there "was a Latino Republican in the House who represented his constituents well, although the main difference is ideology."[31] His perception is that the Republican conservative ideology would make it difficult for a Latino to represent his poorer Latino constituents. Massachusetts Representative Jeffrey Sánchez put it this way: "on the social issues, maybe. When I fought for same-sex marriage, many of the Latino organizations were upset with me, although I've been working on gaining their support on the whole range of issues."[32] Sánchez was able to focus on issues that his Latino constituents could agree on while at the same time support positions that many of his Latino constituents did not support. In a similar way, Texas Senator Leticia van de Putte believes that Latino Republicans "may do well on the moral issues, but on education, health care, and college loans, they do nothing but vote to cut these programs."[33] On the other hand, Michigan Senator Valde García believes that a "Latino Democrat would be more partisan than me. Politicians always talk about the high school dropout rate problem, but we need to do something about it. What have Latino politicians done?"[34] Connecticut Representative Juan Candelaria believes that Latino Republicans can relate to other Latinos, but Democrats "care more about the community, progress, education, breaking the cycle of poverty, the American Dream, and empowering constituents."[35] Partisanship matters even for those who argue that opposite-party coethnics can represent Latino constituents.

Of those who do not believe that opposite-party coethnics would represent Latino constituents well, political philosophy and class status

[31] Personal Interview, November 2007.
[32] Personal Interview, November 2007.
[33] Personal Interview, November 2005.
[34] Personal Interview, November 2007.
[35] Personal Interview, November 2006.

were cited as prominent reasons. Colorado Representative Rafael Gallegos believes that "Republican Latinos would have different philosophical views and differences especially regarding economic opportunity."[36] Connecticut Representative Minnie González puts it bluntly: "Republicans are for the wealthy, and based on my experience there are significant ideological differences."[37] Rhode Island Representative Grace Díaz also sees Republicans as agents of the wealthy: "The Chamber of Commerce is very active and the Republican Governor is in favor of the wealthy. Latinos know that I am there to represent them against the economically powerful."[38]

Conclusion

Former Speaker of the House Tip O'Neill used to say that "all politics is local." In this sample of Latino state legislators, this is readily apparent. Although there are a host of issues that nearly all Latinos particularly care about, like language policy and education, some local communities have particular issues unique to them, like water rights in New Mexico or economic development in suburban Wichita, Kansas. These Latino legislators could not have come from different districts, yet at the same time they have a common bond that transcends party, class, or region. As Schmidt et al. (2000) observe, "to the extent that Latina/o elected officials and political activists can find common ground and common identity, panethnic unity may bring both symbolic and material rewards." It is for this reason that organizations encouraging participation from Latinos of all political parties, lifestyles, and regions are formed to cultivate leadership skills and promote a broad political agenda.

Latino legislators come from a variety of different backgrounds, and most first became involved in politics through the labor movement, volunteering for other candidates, or for personal/issue-based reasons. Unlike African Americans, no Latino legislators indicated that they became involved in politics through church activities. By far the most common method of getting involved in politics is by volunteering for other candidates and establishing networks at that point. The labor movement has also been particularly important for Latinos, and many saw César Chávez as an example of someone who could have easily been involved in politics

---

[36] Personal Interview, November 2005.
[37] Personal Interview, November 2006.
[38] Personal Interview, November 2007.

if he wanted it. Chávez, however, committed to the United Farm Workers struggle and never pursued a career in elective office. Nonetheless, several legislators began their political careers in the labor movement. Some legislators indicated personal frustrations with government or a strong desire to make a difference as their starting points.

Legislators often perceive their districts to be competitive. This is for several reasons, including the uncertainty of pleasing one's constituents and their potential preferences (Arnold 1990). On the other hand, some legislators report that they receive no significant challenges, in either the primary or general election. The real competition for most legislators takes place in primaries. On the other hand, some districts are truly competitive, like Florida Representative Darren Soto's I-4 corridor Orlando district or Utah Representative Mark Wheatley's Utah district.

Latino legislators often describe their districts by referring to the partisan makeup, the economic class of the citizens, and/ or the geographic makeup of the district. Latino legislators represent a wide variety of districts ranging from heavily Republican districts in rural Georgia to heavily Democratic districts in urban Los Angeles. Whereas most Latino legislators represent self-described "working class" districts, some districts are upper middle class and wealthy. Some Latino legislators represent mostly rural districts in the West, whereas others represent urban districts in the Midwest and Northeast.

Although Latino legislators do care about "Latino issues," most identify other issues as more pressing or time consuming.[39] Local issues matter, such as gang violence in urban Atlanta, Georgia, or water rights in rural New Mexico. Health care issues emerged as important priorities for Latino legislators, especially armed forces veterans' health issues. Public safety was also a major concern for Latinos representing mostly urban districts, where violent crime is more salient than in the rural West. By far the most time-consuming issue, however, was the budget, which, after all, is the bottom line.[40] Legislators attempt to bring home the goods for their district and make sure their constituents are given a fair distribution from the state.

Most Latino legislators perceived their ethnicity as a plus when it comes to representing their constituents. Even those who thought non-Latino legislators could adequately represent Latinos conceded that it

---

[39] "Latino issues" means issues that disproportionately affect the Latino community, like education, immigration, and language-related policy.

[40] The budgetary process varies by state and can include a variety of policy dimensions.

TABLE 5.1. *Descriptive Statistics of Interview Subjects*

Ethnic Breakdown	N	Percentage
Mexican American	11	48
Puerto Rican	6	26
Cuban American	2	9
Dominican	3	12
Other	1	4
Partisanship	**N**	**Percentage**
Democratic	19	83
Republican	4	17
Region	**N**	**Percentage**
Northeast	11	48
West	8	27
Southeast	1	4
Midwest	3	12
Chamber	**N**	**Percentage**
Lower	15	65
Upper	8	35
Gender	**N**	**Percentage**
Male	19	82
Female	4	18

would be more difficult for them to do so. Most cited familiarity with the Latino culture and language as the key mechanism for the trust between them and their constituents (Mansbridge 1999). Most pointed to their backgrounds and life experiences as heavily influencing how they see their representative duties (Burden 2007). Some also thought that as Latino legislators, the notion of empowerment matters. That is, Latinos feel more empowered as political agents when one like them has achieved political power and importance (Pantoja and Segura 2003).

Partisanship does matter for Latino legislators. In line with the past couple of decades of political polarization (at least at the elite level), Latino legislators do identify with one of the two political parties and are often committed members (Fiorina et al. 2005). Most Latino legislators argued that a Latino member of the opposite party could not represent their constituents as well. Most cited the other party's major shortcomings as reasons for this. For many Democratic legislators, Republicans were seen as the party of the wealthy and privileged, and since most Latinos do not fall into those categories, it would be exceedingly difficult, if not impossible, for adequate representation.

6

Roll Call Voting Behavior of Latino Legislators

Do Latino members of Congress and state legislators vote differently than their non-Latino counterparts? If so, what are the implications for representative democracy? Do Latino legislators vote differently across states and chambers? If so, what are some of the reasons for this? Does the percentage of Latinos and African Americans in a district make a difference in terms of how members of Congress and legislators vote? Whereas the bulk of the literature on Latino representation has examined roll call voting patterns at the national level, very little attention has been given to examining the roll call voting patterns of Latino state legislators.

This chapter examines the roll call voting behavior of Latino legislators in Colorado, New Jersey, and Texas and compares how Latinos in Congress and in their respective states vote in legislative institutions, using new data from Nolan McCarty's research on state legislative polarization as well as the McCarty, Poole, and Rosenthal NOMINATE data used in many research studies. Although not one of the seven states thoroughly discussed previously, Colorado's recent political transformations make it an exciting state to study. Through the examination of key roll call votes cast by members of Congress from districts with similar proportions of Latinos, it is possible to make some conclusions regarding substantive representation. Even though previous studies have found that the percentage of Latinos makes no difference in the roll call voting patterns of members of Congress, new evidence suggests that in some states, the Latino population is beginning to exert influence, suggesting the continued mainstreaming of Latinos in American society.

Background of Latinos in Colorado, New Jersey, and Texas

The state of Colorado has witnessed a burgeoning Latino population in the past decade, more so than most other states. Eighteen percent of the population is Latino, making it among the ten most populous Latino states. Although only 9 percent of the state's registered voters are Latino, the influence of Latinos in the Colorado electorate cannot be underestimated. In 2004, the state elected Democratic Attorney General Ken Salazar as it's first-ever Latino U.S. senator. At the same time, Salazar's brother, Democrat John Salazar, was elected to Congress as the only Latino House member from the state. The Salazar brothers are moderate Democrats who won by appealing to a conservative white electorate, and in the case of Ken Salazar's election, an electorate in which 19 percent of Latino registered voters are Republican. In the state legislature, Latino descriptive representation is in the single digits. Latinos comprise 6 percent of the Colorado Senate (two members) and 11 percent of the Colorado House of Representatives (seven members).

The influx of Latinos into New Jersey is a relatively recent phenomenon. In 1970, Latinos numbered 4 percent of the population, whereas in 2004, Latinos numbered 14 percent. The growing number of immigrants from Mexico and Central America seeking better economic opportunities explains much of this increase. At the same time, the Puerto Rican and Cuban-American communities in the state are large and better established. Puerto Ricans first began arriving in New Jersey in the 1950s, whereas Cuban Americans came in the 1960s and 1970s (Connors and Dunham 1993). According to the American Community Survey, the Latino Voting Age Population (VAP) stood at 13 percent of the total in 2000, whereas the Latino citizen VAP stood at 9.4 percent of the total in 2000. In other words, of the 14 percent of the New Jersey population that is of Latino heritage, approximately five percentage points are not U.S. citizens (this includes documented and undocumented workers).

Texas is the state with the third-largest percentage of Latinos, who make up 34 percent of the population. Although not yet a majority-minority state like California, many scholars estimate that it is only a matter of time before Texas becomes one. In the 2002 elections, Texas Democrats nominated Latino Tony Sánchez for governor and African-American Mayor Ron Kirk of Dallas for the U.S. Senate. Even though both men lost, to Rick Perry and John Cornyn, respectively, it was the first time that Texas Democrats nominated minority candidates for both offices in a single year, suggesting the growing power of minorities in the state. In 2008, Latino state House member Rick Noriega won the Democratic nomination to challenge U.S. Senator John Cornyn in his re-election bid. Texas, then, is an important state to consider in terms of Latino politics due to its large Latino population and long-term history of Latino involvement in politics.

Theories about African-American representation in Congress cannot be applied to Latinos for a variety of reasons. Latinos are not politically monolithic, nor are they as strongly partisan. It is true that the majority of Latinos identify with the Democratic Party, but a significantly larger percentage of Latinos have been willing to cross party lines in certain elections, such as the election of Michael R. Bloomberg as Mayor of New York City in 2001, when Bloomberg received 48 percent of the Latino vote. Similarly, President Bush received approximately 35 percent of the Latino vote in the 2000 election – far from a majority, but much higher than the low single digits he received from African Americans.

Latinos are also not monolithic when it comes to issue salience and public opinion attitudes. Cuban Americans place a greater value on foreign-policy issues than other Latinos and are more likely to make vote choices on this basis. There are also significant differences among Latinos on policy issues. For example, Puerto Ricans claim to be more pro-life than Cuban Americans, yet they are more Democratic (Uhlaner and García 2002). Immigration attitudes are not uniformly consistent in the Latino community either. Sizeable minorities of Latinos favor "get tough" approaches on immigration, contrary to conventional wisdom. These are but a few examples of the diversity within the Latino community on a host of policy issues (Leal 2007).

To date, scholars have done very little research regarding Latino representation in the U.S. Congress. Virtually no scholars have examined roll call voting in state legislatures because of the dearth of systematic data (Morehouse and Jewell 2004). Existing research on Congress addresses the question of substantive and descriptive representation by examining key roll call votes compiled by the Southwest Voter Research Institute (SWVRI) and the National Hispanic Leadership Agenda (NHLA). Especially given the population boom of Latinos in just the past few years, more research on this subject using new data is clearly warranted.

To what extent does having a Latino/a representative make a difference in terms of substantive representation? An analysis of roll call data can shed light on the differences, if any, among representatives' voting patterns, and it can provide insights into the normative question of whether

Latino elected officials are essential to advancing a Latino agenda. For example, recall Kansas Republican Representative Mario Goico's description of how he helped defeat a bill that would have barred noncitizens from receiving in-state tuition in Kansas colleges and universities. This suggests that the presence of Latinos in legislative institutions can alter in significant ways the outcome of certain pieces of legislation. These types of occurrences, of course, are not captured in most roll call voting data analyses, yet at the same time an exploration of roll call voting can provide glimpses into the nature of representation in legislative institutions across the United States.

What We Know About Latino Roll Call Voting Behavior

The literature on the question of Latino representation in the U.S. Congress is quite sparse, although several studies have been done in recent years. The earliest work on Latino representation borrowed heavily from previous work on African-American representation in Congress. As such, Latinos were assumed to be a group generally more liberal than whites. Welch and Hibbing (1984) noted that Latino Conservative Coalition scores were more liberal than non-Latino representative scores. Their study, however, only classified members from 1973 to 1980. It was not until 1992 that Mexican Americans, Puerto Ricans, and Cuban Americans were to be simultaneously represented in Congress. Earlier Latino representatives were Mexican Americans who had largely entered politics through the Civil Rights Movement and alliance with progressive causes.

Hero and Tolbert (1995) go beyond Welch and Hibbing's (1984) earlier analysis by using SWVRI scores for the 100th Congress to study the representation of Latinos and their interests. In their analysis, Hero and Tolbert find that high SWVRI scores for Latino representatives were not significantly different from non-Latino representatives. In essence, they find that Latinos benefit from collective representation, and that dyadic representation is not evident. Kerr and Miller (1997) respond to this article by arguing that dyadic representation of Latino interests is present. For them, "dyadic and collective representation can and do occur simultaneously in the political system and, as an analytical matter, should be considered together" (Kerr and Miller 1997: 1071). Although exposing some of the methodological problems with the article, Kerr and Miller do not provide the necessary prescriptions for a better analysis.

For example, the SWVRI scores in question are few in number and only cover the 100th Congress.

More recently, Knoll (2009) has examined Latino substantive representation using NHLA scores as the dependent variable. His analysis corroborates Hero and Tolbert (1995) as does the analysis presented here. Knoll (2009) also finds that "Latinos are largely substantively represented by Democrats and majority-Democratic districts or states." One of the problems with using SWVRI and NHLA scores is that only a handful of selected roll call votes are selected, thus biasing any regression estimates. For example, the NHLA takes a position of "no" on the "Marriage Protection Act, HR 3313," which is arguably at odds with public opinion among the Latino rank and file. Latino public opinion on social issues such as gay marriage and abortion are to the right of elite Latino opinion on these issues, leading to problems in efforts to create reliable voting scores.

David Lublin, however, uses Poole-Rosenthal NOMINATE scores in his analysis as his dependent variable. Poole-Rosenthal scores do a much better job of measuring the political ideology of members of Congress because all votes are included, not just a few select votes, such as ADA or ACU scores. The Poole-Rosenthal scores are also continuously distributed, unlike interest group ratings, thus yielding a "true" ideological score for all members rather than a self-selected sample (Lublin 1997). Lublin interacts Latino population with the party of the representative and finds that Republican members are more conservative and Democrats are significantly more liberal when they have higher Latino populations in their districts (Canon 1999a; Lublin 1997). Lublin explains this by noting the differences in who Democrats represent (Mexican Americans, Puerto Ricans) and who Republicans generally represent (Cuban Americans). As Canon (1999b) notes, Lublin does not control for these constituency differences within the Latino community. Notwithstanding such limitations, the data are more comprehensive and systematic, which leads to better insights into the nature of Latino representation.

This chapter updates Lublin's study by examining Latino roll call voting in the late 1990s and beyond for both Congress and several state legislatures. This chapter will test the following hypotheses:

Latino Constituency Effect: As the percentage of Latinos/Latino citizens in a district increases, the ideology of the legislator becomes more liberal.

Latino Legislator Effect: Non-Cuban Latino representatives are more likely to be associated with more liberal ideological scores.

African-American Effect: As the percentage of African Americans in a district increases, the ideology of the legislator (Latino or non-Latino) becomes more liberal.

Partisan Effect: Democratic legislators are more likely to be associated with more liberal ideological scores.

Data and Methods

David Lublin organized the dataset used in the analysis for the U.S. House. This dataset includes Poole-Rosenthal scores and additional population variables.[1] In addition, demographic variables concerning U.S. House districts from the 87th through the 104th Congress are also included. Poole-Rosenthal DW-NOMINATE scores for the 102nd Congress through the 104th Congress have been added to the Lublin data in order to provide for a more updated analysis.[2] Important variables to notice in this dataset include dummy variables for Cuban-American, Mexican-American, and Puerto Rican representatives.[3] Lublin's dataset also includes the demographic population data for these districts, including racial and ethnic background, median family income, and urban population. This dataset is the most updated and comprehensive available for studying Latino representation.

I organized the dataset used in this analysis for state-level legislative scores. McCarty (2005) generously provided NOMINATE scores for each state representative in the states of Colorado (1999), New Jersey (2002), and Texas (2001). I matched the NOMINATE score to the demographic characteristics of the legislator's district based on the dataset I compiled for previous analyses (see Chapter 3).[4] For Colorado, I created a new dataset by contacting Molly Otto from the Legislative Council of the State of Colorado, who generously provided demographic data broken down by district, which I entered into a database. Because of Colorado and Texas' predominantly Mexican-American population, I did not distinguish among Cuban-American, Puerto Rican, or Mexican-American

---

[1] Data analyses conducted using STATA statistical software (Intercooled Stata 7.0).

[2] DW-NOMINATE scores are used in this analysis because such scores are comparable within and across Congresses.

[3] To date, all Latinos elected to the House of Representatives have been Cuban American, Mexican American, or Puerto Rican.

[4] Ideally, I would like to have the voting age population of Latinos in each district for each state, but not every state collects this data, making cross comparisons all the more difficult and problematic. As such, the percentage of Latino citizens in each district is included for Congress and state legislatures.

legislators. Because the Latino members of the New Jersey General Assembly are almost exclusively Puerto Rican, I also did not distinguish among the subethnic groups for that state.

In the regression analysis, the dependent variable is the Poole-Rosenthal DW-NOMINATE ideology scores. As Poole and Rosenthal (1996) note, American politics has become centered on a left-right continuum, especially with regard to income redistribution. Poole and Rosenthal's second dimension revolves around racial issues, but racial issues have been all but submerged into the first dimension in recent years. Poole-Rosenthal scores range from -.851 (for the most liberal member) to .778 (for the most conservative member) from 1971 to 1985. The mean is -.042 for this time period, and the standard around the mean is .30

It would be ideal to have a measure that directly corresponds with Latino interests. Because the Latino community is so diverse, however, it is hard to imagine what such an index would look like. As a result, no such scores have been compiled. The Poole-Rosenthal scores generally correlate with interest group ratings that in many cases measure Latino *economic* interests. Nevertheless, whereas I control for subethnic differences in the subsequent analyses, I do not control for differences within the electorate, including English-language ability and length of time in the country. Such variables cannot be included at the state district level yet, but future research can untangle these distinctions.

Regression analysis is used to analyze these scores relative to the ethnicity of the representative and the population of Latinos and Latino citizens in House districts. Recall that previous studies have used the SWVRI scores and NHLA scores as the dependent variable to assess Latino representation (Hero and Tolbert 1995; Knoll 2009). Poole-Rosenthal scores can help as a better measure here. Since Hero and Tolbert use data from the 100th Congress, this regression analysis tabulates Poole-Rosenthal scores for that Congress alone. Hero and Tolbert use a threshold of at least 5 percent Latinos in a given district to reduce the number of representatives in the sample, which is why the N is 127 instead of 435. This is the baseline of comparison to determine whether Latino substantive representation is present, in that during the 100th Congress the national Latino percentage hovered around 5 percent.

Findings

The first regression analysis (presented in Appendix D) gauges the impact of Cuban-American, Mexican-American, and Puerto Rican representatives on the Poole-Rosenthal first dimension score, not the SWVRI score. Explanatory variables include Cuban-American representative (coded as 1 if Cuban, 0 otherwise), Mexican-American representative (coded as 1 if Mexican, 0 otherwise), Puerto Rican representative (coded as 1 if Puerto Rican, 0 otherwise), percent urban, percent African American, median family income, and political party. As Hero and Tolbert (1995) note, these explanatory variables all might have an impact on ideology.

The coefficient for Mexican-American representative is -.116, whereas the coefficient for Puerto Rican representative is -.318, which suggests that Mexican-American and Puerto Rican representatives have Poole-Rosenthal ideology scores to the left of other members of Congress.[5] Puerto Rican members of Congress had significantly more liberal scores, probably because the districts they represent include high percentages of African Americans as well (e.g., Herman Badillo in New York). Thus, the analysis so far provides strong support for the Latino legislator hypothesis. These findings also corroborate Hero and Tolbert's findings for the 100th Congress, despite the different dependent variable and the separation of Mexican-American and Puerto Rican representatives.

The political party of the member is the strongest predictor of ideology. The percentage of Latinos in the district is not a significant predictor of ideology, unlike the percentage of African Americans in a district. Thus far, these findings are not altogether different from previous findings in the field. Based on these data, one can conclude that there is little evidence of direct substantive representation for Latinos in the 100th Congress. On the other hand, these results do provide evidence of direct substantive representation for African Americans, indicating strong support for the African-American constituency hypothesis and its expectation that higher African-American populations will be associated with more liberal legislator scores.

A further analysis (see Appendix D) involves the same dependent and explanatory variables but does so over the period of the 87th–104th Congresses. Presumably, over time, and utilizing more data, the results may vary, and we may indeed find substantive representation of Latino interests. The coefficients for Mexican-American and Puerto Rican representatives are statistically significant, indicating that they are more likely to be on the more liberal side of the spatial Poole-Rosenthal score.

[5] There are no observations for Cuban-American representatives because none existed at the time of the 100th Congress. Portuguese-American representatives [former Representatives Tony Coelho (D-CA) and Devin Nunes (R-CA)] are not included as Latino representatives. White representatives are the excluded category.

African-American representatives are most liberal, followed by Puerto Rican representatives, and then Mexican-American and Cuban-American representatives. These findings, like the ones for the 100th Congress, provide strong support for the Latino legislator effect.

The findings are most counterintuitive for Cuban representatives, who are typically perceived to be significantly right wing. In fact, such legislators may be hawkish on foreign-policy issues, but when it comes to redistribution and welfare, Cuban-American representatives are sometimes likely to vote with their other Latino colleagues. In addition, all of the other explanatory variables are statistically significant. Other than the percentage Latino variable, the only explanatory variable that is not statistically significant is that of Cuban Representative. The coefficients for Cuban Representative is -.076, which indicates that Cuban-American representatives are more conservative than their Latino counterparts but still are not as conservative as one might expect given the Cuban-American community's reputation for dogmatic conservatism.[6]

Like the results for the 100th Congress, the percentage of Latinos in the district is unrelated to the ideology of members of Congress. Like previous work, I find little evidence of direct, substantive representation of Latinos over this time period. As expected, the political party of the legislator remains a significant variable, suggesting the increasing polarization of the American political parties.

Percent African American is statistically significant, as well as median family income. African Americans have experienced more substantive representation over this time period. The percentage of African Americans in a district is positively associated with more liberal voting scores for representatives of any race. Most importantly, however, is the percentage Latino in district variable that still has no significant effect on Poole-Rosenthal ideology scores, suggesting no support for the Latino constituency hypothesis.

Are these patterns unique to the U.S. Congress? The next set of analyses examines similar questions for the Texas House of Representatives in 2001.[7] The two institutions are similar in many ways yet also exhibit

---

[6] When a regression is performed on all districts with at least a 5 percent Latino population (i.e., excluding districts with virtually no Latinos), the coefficient for Cuban representative becomes significant in the liberal direction, providing even further support to this counterintuitive finding. I had expected a positive significant coefficient for Cuban representative given the alleged conservatism of Cuban American representatives.

[7] The following analyses use data generously provided in part by Professor Nolan McCarty. Unfortunately, state legislative district-level data is limited, and I am unable to control for

some important differences. Texas legislators rarely meet, and its legislature is not nearly as professionalized as in New York or Michigan. The Texas House is composed of thirty-one Latinos, or 21 percent of the body, which is substantially below the 32 percent of Latinos in the state. This is not unusual. Only New Mexico's lower chamber has a higher percentage of Latinos in the House than in the state population, but ironically, it has had no Latino members of the U.S. Congress since Bill Richardson served in the early 1990s.

Table 6.1 provides evidence to support the Latino constituency hypothesis for the Texas House. That is, the proportion of Latino citizens in a district is significantly associated with a more liberal NOMINATE score.[8] Being a Latino representative makes no difference for ideology scores when considered jointly with the proportion of Latino citizens. The proportion African American is nonetheless a significant predictor of the ideology of Texas House members in the full model. These findings suggest that Texas House districts with increasing numbers of Latino citizens are more likely to be associated with liberal ideological scores. The proportion of Latino citizens in a district is significantly related to the ideological score of representatives. The proportion of African Americans in a district is significant, suggesting that the greater the proportion of African Americans in a district, the more likely the representative is to be liberal.[9] The political party of the representative (coded 1 as Republican and 0 as Democrat for this model) is positively, albeit insignificantly, associated with the ideology score.

In the bivariate model for the 1999 Colorado legislature, the proportion of Latino citizens in a district does not significantly affect a legislator's NOMINATE score. This finding is in contrast to the Texas House. In a multivariate model, it turns out that the only significant predictor of a Colorado legislator's NOMINATE score is the political party of the member. Republicans are more likely to be associated with higher (conservative) voting scores, given the polarization of the American political parties in recent years. The presence of a Latino legislator does

income, percent urban, and other variables. I hope that future data will be able to address these concerns.

[8] Separate regression results with the proportion of Latinos in a district (citizens and non-citizens) demonstrate significant results.

[9] In a regression model that omits the proportion Latino in a district in order to rule out possible multicollinearity, the proportion African-American variable is in the correct direction, although not significant. The substantive finding for Latino representative, however, remains the same.

TABLE 6.1. *Impact of Latino Representative and Percent Latino on Poole-Rosenthal Scores for Texas House, Colorado Legislature, New Jersey Legislature, and U.S. House, 1999–2002*

District	TX	CO	NJ House	NJ Senate	U.S. House
Latino	−.249	−.329	−.055	−.112	.322*
Representative	(.186)	(.285)	(.146)	(.250)	(.152)
Proportion	−1.33***	1.33	1.24*	2.01	−.308
Latino Citizen	(.372)	(.842)	(.530)	(1.14)	(.284)
Proportion Black	−1.99***	−.654	1.01**	2.19***	.137
	(.356)	(1.05)	(.352)	(.597)	(.166)
Party of Member	.183	−.442**	−.648***	−.187	.154***
	(.096)	(.155)	(.097)	(.192)	(.050)
Senator	−	−.287*	−	−	−
		(.144)			
Constant	.556***	−.249	.332***	.123	−.038
	(.127)	(.187)	(.107)	(.221)	(.054)
Adjusted R-squared	.37	.16	.78	.62	.04
N	149	96	55	34	426
N of Latinos	27	10	6	0	22

***$p<=.001$; **$p<=.01$; *$p<=.05$.

not significantly affect the ideology voting score. Political party of the member, however, trumps ethnicity in both cases. In a full model incorporating the proportion Latino and a Latino representative (correlated at .55), the political party of the legislator remains the most powerful and significant predictor of the voting scores. Additionally, there is a chamber effect such that lower-chamber members are more likely to have liberal voting scores. Chamber effects have not been strong predictors of the election of Latinos to legislative districts (see Chapter 3), but in Colorado, it appears that senators must be more moderate because of the more heterogeneous and large senate districts.[10] More research on the determinants of the election of Latinos to the Colorado legislature is needed, however, to ascertain such effects.

In the New Jersey Assembly in 2002, the bivariate model shows strong support for the contention that the proportion of Latino citizens in a district will be significantly associated with liberal voting scores. These results are similar to the Texas House. Recall that in New Jersey,

[10] In a regression model omitting the proportion Latino in district, the Senate variable is not significant, although it is in the correct direction, suggesting that more work is needed to assess whether chamber effects affect roll call voting.

legislators are elected from multimember districts, whereby the state is only divided into thirty districts that elect two lower-chamber members and one senator. The proportion African American and the party of the assembly member have the strongest relationship to the ideology of the representative, whereas being a Latino legislator is not significantly associated with voting scores. This stands in contrast to Colorado, where the African-American populations are not as high. In New Jersey, the parties are strong and county party leaders have a say in who runs on the party ticket (three candidates running together for the three legislative seats). As the proportion of Latino citizens in a district rises, liberal ideology scores rise.

In the New Jersey Senate, the findings are somewhat different for the multivariate models. Neither the party of the senator nor the proportion of Latino citizens in a district is a significant predictor of ideology scores for New Jersey senators. Like Colorado, there appears to be a difference in terms of the chamber. Senators are much more responsive to African-American constituencies because of their increased voting participation in key parts of the state.

In the 108th Congress, the presence of a Latino representative is associated with higher NOMINATE scores. In a regression (not shown) that separates Cuban-American, Mexican-American, and Puerto Rican representatives, none of the variables are significant. Consistent with previous analyses, the proportion of Latino citizens makes no difference in terms of voting scores, although somewhat surprisingly, the proportion of African Americans also makes no difference in terms of voting scores. Political party remains a robust predictor of voting, as is the median income of a district, lending support to recent observations of partisan polarization in Congress (McCarty, Poole, and Rosenthal 2007; Theriault 2009).

Conclusion

Given the rapidly growing numbers of Latinos in the United States, this study has attempted to determine the extent to which Latinos are substantively represented in Congress and several state legislatures. In the 100th Congress, the findings of Hero and Tolbert coincided with the findings here. Apparently, the SWVRI scores, albeit limited, were correlated with the Poole-Rosenthal ideology scores, which are the most comprehensive available. For the 87th–104th Congresses and the three state legislatures, however, the results are different: Whether or not a Latino representative represents a constituency has a nil effect on the Poole-Rosenthal score.

However, in the 107th Congress (2002), being a Latino representative has a significant effect on voting scores. Hero and Tolbert (1995) found no significance for a Latino representative in their analysis. By interpreting the coefficient for a Latino representative as insignificant, Hero and Tolbert "conclude that dyadic substantive representation of Hispanics is lacking" (Kerr and Miller 1997: 1067). Analyzing data from all districts for the 87th–104th Congresses, the results show strong effects of all the explanatory variables except the percent Latino in a district. As the proportion of Latino citizens in a district increases, there is a significant liberal effect on the ideology of the Texas House member and the New Jersey Assembly member.

What, then, are some of the normative implications of these analyses? Latinos suffer from a lack of descriptive representation at all levels of government. To what extent is it important that other Latinos represent Latinos? This question deserves additional research that should include public opinion data on how important it is to Latinos that their representatives are like them. In addition, my analysis shows that percentage of Latinos or Latino citizens in U.S. House districts does little to affect ideology scores, but this is different for the Texas House and the New Jersey Assembly, suggesting that state legislators may be more responsive to minority constituents because of the more homogenous and often majority-minority districts. State legislatures also vary in terms of their procedures and partisan influence. Party elites control some more rigidly than others. Chambers may also have different dynamics across and within states. Because of these inter- and intrastate differences, we should expect variations. The presence of Latino representatives makes no difference in voting patterns for any of the legislative bodies except for the U.S. House in one Congress. Latino citizens apparently do not experience greater degrees of direct substantive representation when they elect Latino representatives as opposed to non-Latino representatives. Without concluding that Latino substantive representation is not present, it is safe to conclude that substantive representation of Latino interests is not at the same level as African Americans, for example, although this clearly varies by state. Beside the addition of more states, it will be necessary to do more to compare the African-American population to determine the similarities and differences of these two communities (Casellas 2009b; McClain et al. 2006).

7

Conclusion

Since 2000, the Latino vote has taken on an increased importance in national elections. Presidential candidates from George W. Bush to Barack Obama have made considerable efforts to appeal to this important voting bloc through media advertisements and "get out the vote" efforts. In 2008, New Mexico Governor Bill Richardson became the first major Latino candidate to run for president of the United States and remains the most influential Latino leader in America. Moreover, President Obama made history when he nominated a Latina, Sonia Sotomayor to the U.S. Supreme Court in 2009. Where are the twenty-first-century Latino leaders going to come from? In state legislatures across the country, Latinos are increasingly making their presence known. It is from these state legislatures that the next Latino governor, U.S. Senator, or President of the United States will likely emerge. As such, it is all the more important and timely to understand the conditions under which Latinos are elected to these legislative institutions. This is the first book to demonstrate that Latino representation is shaped not merely by demographic increases, but also by important institutional differences among state legislatures.

As the 2010 Census ends and redistricting commissions begin to draw legislative districts, scholars and policy makers can turn to the findings in this book to ascertain the probability of electing Latinos in districts based on the percentage of Latinos and Latino citizens in such districts. Gerrymandering and the creation of majority-minority districts are controversial and increasingly regulated by the courts. Although Latinos have no doubt benefited from the creation of majority-minority districts, more Latino candidates are emerging to win in districts in which they have no natural advantage. But we must also look beyond the outdated concept of majority-minority districts given that in many cases, Latinos have joined forces with white voters to elect candidates of choice. This is not to say that black-brown coalitions are absent, but the preponderance of evidence indicates that Latino candidates are winning in districts with either Latino majorities or Latino and white combined majorities (Casellas 2009b). This trend is also true in statewide races, such as Florida where Republican Marco Rubio is a leading contender for the U.S. Senate and Nevada where Republican Brian Sandoval is a leading contender for governor.

Legislatures *and* Legislators Matter

The evidence suggests that Latino candidates benefit from higher percentages of Latino citizens in the state, states that are more liberal, and the presence of citizen legislatures. As the fastest-growing and largest ethnic group in the United States, what types of legislative institutions are most conducive to Latino success? Latino candidates have been elected more readily in states with so-called "citizen" legislatures. Highly professional legislatures, like those in New York and Michigan, are not conducive to the election of Latino candidates for several reasons. First, because they meet all year long and the salaries are high, professional legislators have an incentive to remain in office. Second, because citizen legislators have low rates of pay and only meet part-time, they are more conducive to the election of Latino candidates. Such legislators have an incentive to serve for a short time and move on to lobbying, thus opening up previously entrenched seats to political newcomers. Latinos have also been relatively successful in states that have more open seats because of voluntary retirements.

Not only do legislatures matter, but the presence of Latinos serving in legislatures also makes a difference in roll call voting. Latino legislators behave and vote differently compared with their similarly situated non-Latino counterparts. Statistical results demonstrate that roll call voting behavior does indeed vary among state legislatures as well as Congress. Because of their larger, more heterogeneous constituencies, state senators are often less responsive to the percentage of Latinos or African Americans in their districts. Lower chamber legislators, however, are more likely to have liberal voting scores as the percentage of Latinos and African Americans increases.

One thing is common to the Colorado, New Jersey, and Texas legislatures and Congress: The political party of the member (Latino or otherwise) is consistently significant, meaning that Democratic members are more likely to have liberal ideology scores and Republican members are more likely to have conservative ideology scores.[1]

Not All States Are Equal: Institutions and Demographics Matter

This book has uncovered significant differences among the states regarding the probability of electing Latinos to state legislatures and Congress. The relationship between the Latino population of a district and the probability of electing a Latino candidate is strong in all states and Congress. Despite this expected finding, the subtleties of the different state legislatures, as well as the impact of other minority populations on the election of Latino candidates, yield several new insights. Despite the normative appeal of biracial coalitions electing Latino and African-American candidates, the evidence suggests that African-American legislators have benefited from Latino constituents, whereas Latino legislators have benefited more from having white constituents. That is, more African-American legislators represent districts with sizeable Latino populations, whereas Latino legislators generally represent either majority-Latino districts or districts with white and Latino majorities. This seems to provide evidence for the assertion that Latinos are like the Irish or Italians of the nineteenth century in that they are beginning to assimilate into the wider culture, and as their incomes rise, so does their assimilation into white neighborhoods (Erie 1988; Hochschild 1998). As such, Latinos who live in white neighborhoods begin to take on the voting characteristics of their neighbors, which is not surprising given what we know about social networks and contextual influences on voting behavior (Huckfeldt and Sprague 1987).

States that have a longer history of political incorporation of Latinos are more favorable for Latino candidates. For example, the legislatures most conducive to the election of Latino candidates are Florida and New Mexico, where Latinos have been part of the political establishment since the early 1960s and the Spanish colonial period, respectively. The majority

---

[1] This provides further evidence for the much-discussed growing political polarization among the elite classes. These findings do not suggest, however, that citizens are increasingly polarized. In fact, Morris Fiorina (2005) has argued that the American public is largely moderate, while elites (i.e., elected officials and pundits) have become increasingly polarized.

of Florida's Latino representatives and voters are of Cuban ancestry. This group is more likely to vote and participate in politics; as Portes (1984) has demonstrated, Cuban Americans have higher incomes and rates of voter participation than any other Latino group. Florida's legislature is a citizen legislature that meets rarely and has low rates of pay. Both political parties have long incorporated Latinos into positions of leadership in New Mexico. Most of New Mexico's Latinos can trace their ancestry back to the Spanish colonial settlers of the sixteenth century and as such are not newcomers in any sense to political organizations. In fact, New Mexicans first advocated the term "Hispanic" in the early nineteenth century so that they could distinguish themselves from the newly arriving Mexican immigrants who were less educated and poorer than they were.

Unlike Florida and New Mexico, California has not had a long history of Latino political incorporation. However, since the early 1990s, Latinos began to win state legislative seats and even captured important leadership positions. For example, in 1996, Cruz Bustamante became the first Latino Speaker of the California General Assembly. In 1998, Antonio Villaraigosa succeeded him in this position and was elected mayor of Los Angeles in 2005. With important posts like these, Latino party leaders have strongly supported other Latino candidates in their legislative races. Further, non-Latino party leaders such as Governor Arnold Schwarzenegger have strongly supported Latino Republicans, like Abel Maldonado, who became the first Latino Republican State Senator in California in 2004, whom he appointed Lieutenant Governor in 2010. Despite the prominence of some Latino Republicans, some argue that Republicans have effectively conceded the Latino vote to Democrats by maintaining conservative positions on amnesty and border security.

Other states have institutional characteristics, such as multimember districts, that essentially prevent the creation of too many majority-minority districts. As a result, scholars have argued that these districting schemes have been detrimental for minority candidates (Gerber et al. 1998; Kousser 1992; Welch 1990). Contrary to this literature, however, Chapter 3 suggests that such districting systems do not create adverse conditions for Latino legislative candidates.

Based on these findings, what are some of the policy implications? First, citizen legislatures are more conducive to the election of Latino candidates. Highly professional legislatures are not conducive to the election of Latino candidates. An institutional change to a citizen legislature would increase the probability of electing Latino candidates. Second, Latino candidates can and often do win in non-Latino majority districts. Third, even though most Latino legislators are elected from majority-Latino districts, the fact is that growing numbers of Latinos are serving in non-Latino districts. In fact, growing numbers of Latinos are getting elected to statewide offices across the United States, even in conservative Republican states.

The Mainstreaming of Latinos in U.S. Legislatures

Latinos are increasingly winning legislative seats in districts without Latino majorities. In fact, majority-white states have elected Latino governors and senators since 2000. New Mexico's majority-white yet substantially Latino population elected Bill Richardson governor in 2002. In 2004, Democrat Ken Salazar and Republican Mel Martínez were both elected to the U.S. Senate from majority-white "red" states (obviously more surprising for Salazar than for Martínez). Their victories are the culmination of a growing trend of Latinos winning in majority-white legislative districts all over America in the unlikeliest of places, including rural Georgia and Wyoming. They have been able to win in such districts by taking advantage of elite-driven methods aimed at ensuring minority representation and by exploiting the features of the electoral system, such as Democratic primaries to win in solidly one-party districts.

The most obvious elite-driven method, however, has been the use of redistricting to help minorities win in friendly districts. This process has proven controversial, especially in the courts that have been skeptical of efforts to use race or ethnicity for drawing legislative districts. However, following *Thornburg v. Gingles* in 1986, many states created majority-minority districts to make it easier for minorities to elect candidates of choice. There is no question that majority-African-American districts created after the 1990 Census helped elect many more African Americans to state legislatures and Congress. After 1992, fifteen majority-black districts and ten majority-Latino districts were created across the country (Tien 2009). In the case of the majority-Latino districts, new Latino leaders were elected to Congress, including Representatives Ileana Ros-Lehtinen (R-FL) and Robert Menéndez (D-NJ). Because the *Shaw* court cases from the 1990s have made it more difficult for race to be used as the sole factor in drawing legislative districts, many majority-minority congressional districts, especially in the South, were dismantled.

African Americans and Latinos

Some scholars had assumed that Latinos were like African Americans in terms of their political behavior, attitudes, and representative styles (Dolbeare 1986). Popular elected officials like Mayor Harold Washington of Chicago, Mayor David N. Dinkins of New York City, President Barack Obama, and Mayor Antonio Villaraigosa of Los Angeles have been able to forge winning coalitions of African Americans, Latinos, and even white voters, but these are exceptions to the rule.

More often, as this book demonstrates, Latinos have been just as successful as African Americans in terms of winning in districts with no clear ethnic advantage, making redistricting less of a necessity for the election of Latino candidates – itself an important empirical finding heretofore undeveloped in the literature on racial and ethnic representation. At the same time, Latinos obviously have greater probabilities of winning in districts with greater percentages of Latino voters, although this varies by state and legislative design.

Party Outreach Extends Beyond Presidential Races

Political parties are strategizing for the long term by supporting Latino candidates early on in order to anticipate the potential Latino majority of the district. In some one-party-dominated districts, the dominant party may take a risk and nominate a minority candidate who is bound to win the election, whereas the weaker party may support a minority candidate to publicly tout its commitment to that particular community. This is an important departure from Paul Frymer's (1999) argument that political parties have been unresponsive to minorities. I agree with Frymer that both political parties have historically been unresponsive to African Americans and Latinos; however, both political parties have clearly sought to reach out to the Latino community in *recent* presidential elections.

Why the change in responsiveness? Republicans in particular see the demographic projections, and want to be able to win future elections (Downs 1957). In order to do this, they must win at least 30 percent of the Latino vote in presidential election years. Since African Americans are reliably Democratic, the Republicans have focused more recently on trying to peel off some Latinos from the Democratic coalition (Fraga and Leal 2004). Because of this increased competition, Democrats have had to respond by re-energizing their outreach efforts to Latinos. Republicans are not helped by policies that alienate the Latino population, including laws such as Arizona's SB 1070, passed in April 2010, which makes it a crime under state law to be in the state illegally – previously only a federal offense. Many Latinos perceive this law as a direct attack on their culture.[2]

An important and novel finding of this book is that party leaders, especially in the Republican Party, have helped ensure Latino representation by actively recruiting Latino candidates to run in safe districts. Five of the Latinos representing non-Latino majority districts are Republicans who were clearly recruited by party leaders to run for office. They are from states as diverse as Georgia and North Carolina and represent conservative, white districts. Democratic Party leaders have been less active in recruiting Latino candidates for the simple fact that most Latino elected officials are Democrats anyway, so there is less of a problem in terms of supply.[3] Secondly, Democratic Party leaders often have to choose between African-American and Latino candidates and do not want to alienate one minority group at the expense of the other. Finally, few majority-white Democratic districts exist outside of the Northeast and West Coast, making it more difficult for Latinos to be recruited by party leaders.

Another factor indicating the mainstreaming of Latinos is the election of Latinos who are not obviously Latino to non-Latino majority districts. This is often the case with married women who take their spouse's name, or Latinos who have Anglo fathers, such as Governor Bill Richardson (D-NM). Depending on the nature of the districts, some Latinos try to advertise their Latino heritage if it will benefit them, whereas others do not advertise their heritage if it might not translate into more votes, suggesting that neither political party is more likely to have candidates with this trait.

The election of Latino candidates to non-Latino majority districts is not just a theoretical possibility. Latino legislators from all corners of the United States are winning legislative seats in places with small Latino populations. Whereas Latinos have long held statewide elected office in New Mexico, we are beginning to see the emergence of a new generation of Latino leaders who are able to transcend ethnicity and win in places previously unavailable to them. It is only a matter of time before a Latino

---

[2] The act requires law enforcement to ask suspected illegal immigrants for proof of citizenship. Critics say it enshrines racial profiling and targets Latino immigrants. Some national Republicans, such as former Florida Gov. Jeb Bush have spoken out against this law.

[3] The supply of candidates varies by region and context, but overall I argue that the Democratic party has a larger supply of candidates than the Republican party.

becomes Mayor of New York City and perhaps even governor in a state other than New Mexico.

Latino Pan-Ethnic Identity Despite District Differences

In terms of political background, Latino legislators described their involvement in politics as stemming from a variety of sources, including volunteering in campaigns, the labor movement, and personal/idiosyncratic reasons. Although some Latino legislators noted historically salient issues like education or immigration, most legislators pointed to budgetary concerns, health care, and public safety issues as occupying more of their time. Latino legislators viewed themselves as better able to represent Latino constituents and provided various examples and reasons for this. For example, Representatives Ileana Ros-Lehtinen and Lincoln Díaz-Balart (R-Florida) both refused to sign the "Contract with America" in 1994 precisely because they deemed some of its components too harsh on immigration. Even among those who thought that non-Latinos could represent Latinos well, they argued that it would be more difficult or challenging. Latino legislators reported a strong sense of pan-ethnic identity, as exemplified by a Cuban-American Republican legislator in Kansas helping kill a bill that would disproportionately affect Mexican-American immigrants. To be sure, partisanship still matters for Latino legislators, with Democratic legislators obviously arguing that Democrats are better representatives of Latino interests. On the other hand, some Democratic legislators acknowledged that Republican Latinos would be better representatives regarding social issues, such as abortion.

Variations in Latino Legislators' Voting Records

Latino legislators have more liberal voting scores than white representatives, but these scores do not capture the full range of issues and only reflect economic policy. Latinos clearly side with the Democratic Party's liberal economic policies, but this does not mean that Latinos are in lockstep with the Democratic Party's views on controversial social issues. These differences need to be disaggregated. For example, Connecticut Representative David Aldarondo's (D) views on same-sex marriage are more conservative than his Democratic colleagues in the Connecticut General Assembly. Additionally, there are some differences among the three major Latino subgroups. Puerto Rican legislators are the most liberal, followed by Mexican Americans and then Cuban Americans. Cuban-American legislators, however, are not nearly as conservative on the Poole-Rosenthal first dimension as one might expect. On economic and immigration policies, Cuban-American representatives are often voting with Democrats, whereas on foreign-policy issues, they are adamant in their opposition to Communist regimes, including China.

The legislative institutions the Founders envisioned have served countless Americans. Since that time, people from all over the world have settled in the United States and have been elected to the very institutions the Founders created. Little did they know that an African American would be elected President of the United States, or a Latina would become Associate Justice of the U.S. Supreme Court, but today we have Americans of various backgrounds serving their peers in the halls of Congress and in state legislatures across the country. Now that Latinos are the largest minority group in the United States, we will undoubtedly experience a new wave of Latinos elected to represent this growing community. There is certainly no shortage of talent within the Latino community, and Americans of all backgrounds can be proud that Latinos, like the Irish, Italian, and Jewish immigrants before them, will achieve the promise of American democracy by full incorporation into the political process.

Appendix A

Robustness Checks

The tests in Chapter 2 were also conducted using various different model specifications to account for possible model-driven results. Tests using traditional ordinary least squares (OLS) models indicate similar substantive results. OLS models 1 through 5 all demonstrate that the percentage Latino in state remains strongly significant across the board. All other variables exhibit similar coefficients, despite the higher standard errors due to autocorrelation. Because OLS assumes independence of the dependent variable, it is an inappropriate method for these data.

Random effects models with both the state and year as the group variables, however, differ in minor ways as explained later. These types of models are appropriate for time-series data but do not account for serial autocorrelation like the feasible generalized least squares (FGLS) procedure (Bertrand et al. 2004). Model 1 is robust across both state and year models. Model 2 with the states as the random effects control indicates the same substantive results with the exception of the implementation of term limits variable, which is not statistically significant, although in the negative direction. This suggests that there are considerable state-to-state differences on the impact of term limits on Latino representation. Model 4 yields the same results for both time and state specifications. Because all other specifications show a strong and significantly negative effect of more professional legislatures on Latino representation, this seems more like a statistical artifact. Overall, the initial results hold well even across a variety of model specifications.

Appendix B

Chapter 3 Basic Models by State
Pre- and Post-2000 Redistricting

TABLE A.1. *Probit Analysis of Latino Representation in New Mexico's Lower Chamber and Entire Legislature, 1991 and 2003*

District	Dependent Variable: Latino Representative = 1			
	LC-2003	EL-2003	LC-1991	EL-1991
Proportion Latino	5.74**	6.04**	6.90**	7.28**
	(1.14)	(.96)	(1.42)	(1.17)
Proportion African	-2.38	-9.42	16.50	13.49
American	(11.01)	(9.55)	(9.59)	(8.16)
Senator	–	-.25	–	-.08
		(.30)		(.34)
Constant	-2.6**	-2.6**	-3.6**	-3.7**
	(.56)	(.48)	(.75)	(.64)
N	70	112	70	112
Pseudo R2	.38	.40	.47	.48
N of Latinos	30	44	27	41

*$p<=.05$; **$p<=.01$ (standard errors in parentheses).

TABLE A.2. *Probability of a Latino Being Elected to the 2003 New Mexico Legislature*

Percentage Latino in District	Probability of Electing a Latino
80	98
60	79
50	57
40	34
20	5

TABLE A.3. *Probit Analysis of Latino Representation in California's Lower Chamber and Entire Legislature, 2000 and 2003*

District	Dependent Variable: Latino Representative = 1			
	LC-2003	EL-2003	LC-2000	EL-2000
Proportion Latino	6.62**	5.38**	13.04**	8.02**
	(1.31)	(.89)	(2.87)	(1.44)
Proportion African	-7.86	-1.92	-2.46	-.45
American	(4.07)	(2.12)	(2.83)	(1.4)
Senator	–	.36	–	-.61
		(.33)		(.34)
Constant	-2.8*	-2.7**	-3.1**	-2.4**
	(.55)	(.42)	(.59)	(.36)
N	80	120	80	120
Pseudo R2	.52	.39	.60	.42
N of Latinos	18	28	16	25

*$p<=.05$; **$p<=.01$ (standard errors in parentheses).

TABLE A.4. *Probability of a Latino Being Elected to the 2003 California Legislature*

Percentage Latino in District	Probability of Electing a Latino
80	95
60	71
50	50
40	30
20	5

Estimates derived from probit results in Equation 2 of Table A.1 (percentage African American and the dummy variable for senator are set at their means).

Estimates derived from probit results in Equation 2 of Table A.3 (percentage African American and the dummy variable for senator are set at their means).

Estimates derived from probit results in Equation 2 of Table A.5 (percentage African American and the dummy variable for senator are set at their means).

Estimates derived from probit results in Equation 2 of Table A.7 (percentage African American and the dummy variable for senator are set at their means).

TABLE A.5. *Probit Analysis of Latino Representation in Texas's Lower Chamber and Entire Legislature, 2001 and 2003*

District	Dependent Variable: Latino Representative = 1			
	LC-2003	EL-2003	LC-2001	EL-2001
Proportion Latino	5.4**	5.4**	4.06**	4.22**
	(.87)	(.77)	(.66)	(.61)
Proportion African American	-.30	-.63	−1.26	-1.44
	(1.78)	(1.67)	(1.72)	(1.65)
Senator	–	.27	–	.28
		(.41)		(.37)
Constant	−3.2**	-3.2**	−2.5**	−2.5**
	(.58)	(.52)	(.43)	(.38)
N	150	181	150	181
Pseudo R2	.61	.60	.48	.49
N of Latinos	30	37	27	34

*$p<=.05$; **$p<=.01$ (standard errors in parentheses).

TABLE A.6. *Probability of a Latino Being Elected to the 2003 Texas Legislature*

Percentage Latino in District	Probability of Electing a Latino
80	87
60	52
50	31
40	15
20	2

TABLE A.7. *Probit Analysis of Latino Representation in Arizona's Lower Chamber and Entire Legislature, 2001 and 2003*

District	Dependent Variable: Latino Representative = 1			
	LC-2003	EL-2003	LC-2001	EL-2001
Proportion Latino	7.2**	6.19*	6.26**	5.88**
	(2.4)	(1.78)	(1.65)	(1.40)
Proportion African American	7.9	11.58	-16.43	-8.40
	(15.1)	(12.7)	(10.95)	(8.96)
Senator	–	-.10	–	-.26
		(.47)		(.46)
Constant	-3.7**	-3.5**	-2.5**	-2.7**
	(.97)	(.72)	(.56)	(.46)
N	60	90	60	90
Pseudo R2	.55	.51	.41	.42
N of Latinos	11	16	10	14

*$p<=.05$; **$p<=.01$ (standard errors in parentheses).

TABLE A.8. *Probability of a Latino Being Elected to the 2003 Arizona Legislature*

Percentage Latino in District	Probability of Electing a Latino
80	96
60	71
50	47
40	25
20	3

TABLE A.9. *Probit Analysis of Latino Representation in Florida's Lower Chamber and Entire Legislature, 1996 and 2003*

District	Dependent Variable: Latino Representative = 1			
	LC-2003	EL-2003	LC-1996	EL-1996
Proportion Latino	14.5*	14.75*	10.3**	10.8**
	(6.0)	(5.83)	(3.6)	(3.6)
Proportion African American	−1.4	−1.38	−3.0	−3.3
	(3.1)	(3.02)	(4.2)	(4.5)
Senator	−	−2.1	−	−1.0(1.75)
		(3.3)		
Constant	−3.6**	−3.6**	−3.1**	−3.1**
	(1.2)	(1.3)	(.85)	(.89)
N	120	160	120	160
Pseudo R2	.90	.92	.88	.90
N of Latinos	13	16	12	15

$*p<=.05$; $**p<=.01$ (standard errors in parentheses).

TABLE A.10. *Probability of a Latino Being Elected to the 2003 Florida Legislature*

Percentage Latino in District	Probability of Electing a Latino
80	99
60	99
50	99
40	94
20	8

TABLE A.11. *Probit Analysis of Latino Representation in New York's Lower Chamber and Entire Legislature, 2003*

District	Dependent Variable: Latino Representative = 1	
	LC-2003	EL-2003
Proportion Latino	2.9**	3.46**
	(.78)	(.69)
Proportion African	-.28	.31
American	(.97)	(.77)
Senator	–	-.08
		(.36)
Constant	-2.1**	-2.3**
	(.29)	(.30)
N	150	212
Pseudo R2	.21	.29
N of Latinos	10	15

*p<=.05; **p<=.01 (standard errors in parentheses).

TABLE A.12. *Probability of a Latino Being Elected to the 2003 New York Legislature*

Percentage Latino in District	Probability of Electing a Latino
80	67
60	40
50	28
40	17
20	5

TABLE A.13. *Probit Analysis of Latino Representation in New Jersey's Lower Chamber and Entire Legislature, 2003*

District	Dependent Variable: Latino Representative = 1	
	LC-2003	EL-2003
Proportion Latino	4.25**	3.98**
	(1.6)	(1.40)
Proportion African	.67	.80
American	(1.76)	(1.59)
Senator	–	–
Constant	-2.3**	-2.5**
	(.52)	(.47)
N	80	120
Pseudo R2	.21	.21
N of Latinos	6	6

*p<=. 05; **p<=.01 (standard errors in parentheses).

TABLE A.14. *Probability of a Latino Being Elected to the 2003 New Jersey Legislature*

Percentage Latino in District	Probability of Electing a Latino
80	89
60	65
50	48
40	32
20	9

TABLE A.15. *Probit Analysis of Latino Representation in the U.S. House, 1995 and 2003*

District	Dependent Variable: Latino Representative = 1	
	LC-2003	LC-1995
Proportion Latino	12.6**	8.81**
	(2.9)	(1.74)
Proportion African-American	-2.2	-2.67
	(3.5)	(2.12)
Constant	-6.7**	-3.7**
	(1.7)	(.67)
N	435	435
Pseudo R2	.86	.75
N of Latinos	22	17

*$p<=.05$; **$p<=.01$ (standard errors in parentheses).

TABLE A.16. *Probability of a Latino Being Elected to the 2003 U.S. House*

Percentage Latino in District	Probability of Electing a Latino
80	99
60	74
50	27
40	3
20	.000056

Estimates derived from probit results in Equation 2 of Table A.9 (percentage African American and the dummy variable for senator are set at their means).

Estimates derived from probit results in Equation 2 of Table A.11 (percentage African American and the dummy variable for senator are set at their means).

TABLE A.17. *Probit Analysis of Latino Representation in Seven State Lower Chambers and the U.S. House, 2003–2004*

District	Dependent Variable: Latino Representative = 1							
	NM	CA	TX	AZ	FL	NY	NJ	USH
Proportion Latino	5.7**	6.6**	5.4**	7.2**	14.5*	2.9**	4.3**	12.6**
	(1.1)	(1.3)	(.87)	(2.4)	(6.0)	(.78)	(1.6)	(2.9)
Proportion Black	-2.4	-7.9	-.30	7.9	-1.4	-.28	.67	-2.2
	(11.0)	(4.1)	(1.8)	(15.1)	(3.1)	(.97)	(1.8)	(3.5)
Constant	-2.6**	-2.8**	-3.2**	-3.7**	-3.6**	-2.1**	-2.3**	-6.7**
	(.56)	(.97)	(.58)	(.97)	(1.2)	(.29)	(.52)	(1.7)
N	70	80	150	60	120	150	80	435
Pseudo R2	.38	.51	.61	.55	.90	.21	.25	.86
N of Latinos	30	18	30	11	13	10	6	22

*$p<=.05$; **$p<=.01$ (standard errors in parentheses).

TABLE A.18. *Probit Analysis of Latino Representation in Five State Lower Chambers and the U.S. House, Pre-2000 Redistricting*

District	Dependent Variable: Latino Representative = 1					
	NM 91	CA 00	TX 01	AZ 00	FL 96	USH 95
Proportion	6.9**	13.0**	4.1**	6.3**	10.3**	8.8**
Latino	(1.4)	(2.9)	(.66)	(1.7)	(3.6)	(1.7)
Proportion	16.5	-2.5	-1.3	-16.4	-3.0	-2.7
Black	(9.6)	(2.8)	(1.7)	(10.9)	(4.2)	(2.1)
Constant	-3.6**	-3.1**	-2.5**	-2.5**	-3.1**	-3.7**
	(.75)	(.59)	(.43)	(.56)	(.85)	(.67)
N	70	80	150	60	120	435
Pseudo R2	.47	.60	.48	.41	.88	.75
N of Latinos	27	16	27	10	12	17

$p<=.05$; **$p<=.01$ (standard errors in parentheses).

TABLE A.19. *Probit Analysis of Latino Representation in Seven State Legislatures, 2003–2004*

District	Dependent Variable: Latino Representative = 1						
	NM	CA	TX	AZ	FL	NY	NJ
Proportion	6.0**	5.4**	5.4**	6.2**	14.8*	3.5**	3.9**
Latino	(1.1)	(.89)	(.77)	(1.8)	(5.8)	(.69)	(1.4)
Proportion	-9.4	-1.9	-.63	11.6	-1.4	.31	.80
Black	(9.6)	(2.1)	(1.7)	(12.7)	(3.0)	(.77)	(1.6)
Senator	-.25	.36	.27	-.10	-2.1	-.08	–
	(.30)	(.33)	(.41)	(.47)	(3.3)	(.36)	
Constant	-2.6**	-2.7**	-3.2**	-3.5**	-3.6**	-2.3**	-2.5**
	(.48)	(.42)	(.52)	(.72)	(1.3)	(.30)	(.47)
N	112	120	181	90	160	212	120
Pseudo R2	.40	.39	.60	.51	.92	.25	.21
N of Latinos	44	29	37	16	16	15	6

$p<=.05$; **$p<=.01$ (standard errors in parentheses).

Estimates derived from probit results in Equation 2 of Table A.13 (percentage African American is set at its mean).

Estimates derived from probit results in Equation 2 of Table A.15 (percentage African American is set at its mean).

Appendix C

Questionnaire

Thank you for agreeing to answer a few questions for my book on representation. This should not take more than fifteen minutes of your time. Of course, there are no right or wrong answers. I am only interested in what you think about your role as a legislator. You may choose not to answer a question if you feel uncomfortable doing so. Your answers will be used in my book. I would like to be able to quote you in my book, but if there are answers that you would like to be held in confidence, please let me know immediately before or after your statement. If you wish to complete this interview anonymously, let me know now.

1. Do you recall when and how you first became involved in elective politics?
2. What was the first office you were elected to? When were you first elected?
3. Did you run for any other office before you became a (current position)?
4. For your current seat, how many times did you run before your first election?
5. Did you defeat an incumbent or win in an open seat contest?
6. What was the name of the individual you defeated? Primary or general?
7. Tell me more about the competitiveness of your district. Do you draw serious challenges every two or four years, or are you in what you consider a safe district? What have been the margins of victory in recent elections?

8. If you have had primary opponents, what kinds of candidates have they been? What about general election opponents? Probe ethnicity, ideology, policy positions.

9. Tell me some more about the district your represent. (Probe ethnicity, rural versus urban, economic class, immigrants.) Is your district heavily (D or R) or divided?

10. Have you thought about running for higher office? If so, what are some of the factors that were instrumental in your decision to run or not to run?

11. Are you currently considering running for higher office? If yes, which one?

12. In your most recently completed legislative session, on what would you say you spent most of your time? On what did you spend the second largest amount of time? Probe time specific. What sorts of actions have you taken beside voting on the floor regarding (issue)?

13. In your opinion, would a white or African American represent your Latino constituents the same way you do?

14. In your opinion, would a Latino (R or D opposite prompt) represent your Latino constituents the same way you do?

15. What do you think would be some of the similarities/differences?

16. What do you want to communicate the most to your constituents about what you do?

17. Is there anything else you would like to add?

Appendix D

TABLE A.20. *Probit Analysis of Latino Representation in Five State Legislatures, Pre-2000 Redistricting*

District	Dependent Variable: Latino Representative = 1						
	NM 91	CA 00	TX 01	AZ 00	FL 96	NY	NJ
Proportion Latino	7.3** (.1.2)	8.0** (1.4)	4.2** (.61)	5.9** (1.4)	10.8** (3.6)	–	–
Proportion Black	13.5 (8.2)	-.45 (1.4)	-1.4 (1.7)	-8.4 (8.9)	-3.3 (4.5)	–	–
Senator	-.08 (.34)	-.61 (.34)	.28 (.37)	-.26 (.46)	-1.0(1.8)	–	
Constant	-3.7** (.64)	-2.4** (.36)	-2.5** (.38)	-2.7** (.46)	-3.1** (.89)	–	–
N	112	120	181	90	160	212	120
Pseudo R2	.48	.42	.49	.42	.90	–	–
N of Latinos	41	25	34	14	15	–	

$*p<=.05; **p<=.01$ (standard errors in parentheses).

Appendix E

TABLE A.21. *Impact of Mexican-American and Puerto Rican Representative and Percent Latino on Poole-Rosenthal Score for the 100th Congress*

Explanatory Variable	
Cuban Representative	–
Mexican Representative	-.116
	(.124)
Puerto Rican Representative	-.318*
	(.152)
African-American Representative	-.639***
	(.091)
Percentage Latino in District	.001
	(.002)
Percentage African American	-.002**
	(.002)
Percentage Urban	-.002*
	(.001)
Median Family Income	-5.11E-06
	(5.3E-06)
Political Party of Member	-1.13***
	(.031)
Constant	.692***
	(.090)
Ajusted R-squared	.81
N	435
N of Latinos	11

***$p<=.001$; **$p<=.01$; *$p<=.05$; (standard errors in parentheses).

TABLE A.22. *Impact of Cuban-American, Mexican-American, and Puerto Rican Representative and Percent Latino on Poole-Rosenthal Score for the 87th–104th Congresses*

Explanatory Variable Model	
Cuban Representative	−.076
	(.147)
Mexican Representative	−.213***
	(.056)
Puerto Rican Representative	−.192***
	(.053)
African-American Representative	−.289***
	(.038)
Percentage Latino in District	−.000
	(.000)
Percentage African – American	−.002***
	(.001)
Percentage Urban	−.003***
	(.000)
Median Family Income	3.44e-06***
	(5.78e-07)
Political Party of Member	−.002**
	(.001)
Constant	.180***
	(.023)
Adjusted R-squared	.12
N	6814

*** $p<=.001$; **$p<=.01$; *$p<=.05$ (standard errors in parentheses).

References

Achen, Christopher, and D. Snidal. 1989. "Rational Deterrence Theory and Comparative Case Studies." *World Politics* 41: 144–69.

Alba, Richard, and V. Nee. 2003. *Remaking the American Mainstream: Assimilation and Contemporary Immigration.* Cambridge, MA: Harvard University Press.

Anderson, David. April 6, 2003. "First Latino Delegate's Life a Whirlwind of Preparation." *Suburban Newsline.*

Arnold, R. Douglas. 1990. *The Logic of Congressional Action.* New Haven, CT: Yale University Press.

Barreto, Matt A., Gary Segura, and Nathan Woods. 2004. "The Mobilizing Effect of Majority-Minority Districts on Latino Turnout." *American Political Science Review* 98: 65–75.

Beck, Nathaniel, and J. Katz. 1995. "What to Do (and Not to Do) with Time-Series Cross-Section Data." *American Political Science Review* 89: 634–47.

Bedoya, Alvaro. 2006. "The Unforeseen Effects of Georgia v. Ashcroft on the Latino Community." *Yale Law Journal* 115: 2112–46.

Berkman, Michael B. 1994. "State Legislators in Congress: Strategic Politicians, Professional Legislatures, and the Party Nexus." *American Journal of Political Science* 38: 1025–55.

Berman, David. 1998. *Arizona Politics and Government: The Quests for Autonomy, Democracy, and Development.* Lincoln, NE: University of Nebraska Press.

Bertrand, Marianne, E. Duflo, and S. Mullainathan. 2004. "How Much Should We Trust Differences-in-Differences Estimates?" *Quarterly Journal of Economics* 2: 249–75.

Bickerstaff, Steve. 2007. *Lines in the Sand: Congressional Redistricting in Texas and the Fall of Tom DeLay.* Austin, TX: The University of Texas Press.

Bobo, Lawrence, and Frank Gilliam. 1990. "Race, Sociopolitical Participation, and Black Empowerment." *American Political Science Review* 84(March): 377–93.

Bratton, Kathleen R. 2006. "The Behavior and Success of Latino Legislators: Evidence from the States." *Social Science Quarterly* 87(December): 1136–57.

Bratton, Kathleen R., and Kerry Haynie. 1999. "Agenda Setting and Legislative Success in State Legislatures: The Effects of Gender and Race." *Journal of Politics* 61(3): 658–79.

Breaux, David., and M. Jewell. 1992. "Winning Big: The Incumbency Advantage in State Legislative Races." In *Changing Patterns in State Legislative Careers*, eds. G. Moncrief and J. Thompson, 87–105. Ann Arbor, MI: University of Michigan Press.

Brockington, David, T. Donovan, S. Bowler, and R. Brischetto. 1998. "Minority Representation Under Cumulative and Limited Voting." *Journal of Politics* 60: 1108–25.

Browning, Rufus P., Dale Marshall, and David Tabb. 1984. *Protest Is Not Enough: The Struggle of Blacks and Hispanics for Equality in Urban Politics*. Berkeley, CA: University of California Press.

Bullock, Charles. 1992. "Minorities in State Legislatures." In *Changing Patterns of State Legislative Leadership*, eds. G. Moncrief and J. Thompson, 39–58. Ann Arbor, MI: University of Michigan Press.

Burden, Barry. 2007. *Personal Roots of Representation*. Princeton, NJ: Princeton University Press.

Burkhart, Michael T. June 17, 2001. "5th District Primary Not Really a Contest." *Courier-Post*.

Burrell, Barbara. 1990. *A Woman's Place Is in the House*. Ann Arbor, MI: University of Michigan Press.

Cain, Bruce E., Kiewiet D. Roderick, and Carole J. Uhlaner. 1991. "The Acquisition of Partisanship by Latinos and Asian Americans." *American Journal of Political Science* 35(2): 390–422.

Cameron, Charles, David Epstein, and Sharon O'Halloran. 1996. "Do Majority-Minority Districts Maximize Substantive Black Representation in Congress?" *American Political Science Review* 90: 794–812.

Canon, David T. 1990. *Actors, Athletes, and Astronauts: Political Amateurs in the United States Congress*. Chicago: University of Chicago Press.

   1999a. *Race, Redistricting, and Representation: The Unintended Consequences of Black Majority Districts*. Chicago: University of Chicago Press.

   1999b. "Electoral Systems and the Representation of Minority Interests In Legislatures." *Legislative Studies Quarterly* 24(3): 331–85.

Carey, John M., R. Niemi, and L. Powell. 2000. "Incumbency and the Probability of Reelection in State Legislative Elections." *Journal of Politics* 62: 671–700.

Carroll, Susan J., and K. Jenkins. 2001. "Increasing Diversity or More of the Same? Term Limits and the Representation of Minorities, Women, and Minority Women in State Legislatures." Paper presented at the American Political Science Association Meeting, San Francisco, California.

Cartagena, Juan. 2004. "Latinos and Section 5 of the Voting Rights Act: Beyond Black and White." *National Black Law Journal* 18: 201–23.

   2005. "New Jersey's Multi-Member Legislative Districts and Latino Political Power." *Rutgers Race and Law Review* 7: 13–50.

Casellas, Jason P. 2009a. "The Institutional and Demographic Determinants of Latino Representation." *Legislative Studies Quarterly* 34: 399–426.

2009b. "Coalitions in the House? The Election of Minorities to State Legislatures and Congress." *Political Research Quarterly* 62(1): 120–31.

Celis, Karen. 2008. "Gendering Representation." In *Politics, Gender, and Concepts: Theory and Methodology*, eds. Amy G. Mazur and Gary Goertz. Cambridge: Cambridge University Press.

Chakraborty, Barnini. February 2, 2003. "Georgia's New Latino Senator Ready to Help." *The State*.

Chan, Sewell. July 30, 2009. "Olga Mendez, 84, Longtime State Senator." *The New York Times*.

Cisse, Elisabeth. May 18, 1998. "Assemblymember Liz Figueroa Eyes State Senate." *The Pioneer*.

Collier, David, and R. Adcock. 1999. "Democracy and Dichotomies: A Pragmatic Approach to Choices about Concepts." *Annual Review of Political Science* 2(1): 537–66.

Conde, Carlos. 1998. "Republicans on the Mend." *Hispanic* 11: 36–42.

Connors, Richard J., and W. Dunham. 1993. *The Government of New Jersey*. Lanham, MD: Rowman and Littlefield.

Copeland, Gary, C. Opheim, and C. Pickthorn. 2004. "Half Empty or Half Full: The Election of Underrepresented Groups to State Legislatures and Career Progression." Paper presented at the 2004 Annual Meeting of the Southwestern Political Science Association, Corpus Christi, Texas.

Cox, Gary, and J. Katz. 1996. "Why Did the Incumbency Advantage in U.S. House Elections Grow?" *American Journal of Political Science* 40: 478–97.

Dahl, Robert. 1961. *Who Governs?* New Haven, CT: Yale University Press.

Dawson, Michael. 1994. *Behind the Mule*. Princeton, NJ: Princeton University Press.

De la Garza, Rodolfo, L. DeSipio, F. C. García, and A. Falcón. 1992. *Latino Voices: Mexican, Puerto Rican, and Cuban Perspectives on American Politics*. Boulder, CO: Westview Press.

De la Garza, Rodolfo O. 1994. *Barrio Ballots: Latino Politics in the 1990 Elections*. Boulder, CO: Westview Press.

De la Garza et al. 1996. "Will the Real Americans Please Stand Up: Anglo and Mexican American Support of Core American Political Values." *American Journal of Political Science* 40(2): 335–51.

DeMasters, Karen. November 2, 1997. "Some Races Matter More Than Others." *The New York Times*.

DeSipio, Louis. 1996. *Counting on the Latino Vote*. Charlottesville, VA: University of Virginia Press.

Dolbeare, Kenneth M. 1986. *Democracy at Risk: The Politics of Economic Renewal*. Chatham, NJ: Chatham House Publishers.

Downs, Anthony. 1957. *An Economic Theory of Democracy*. New York: Harper Press.

Elman, Colin. 2005. "Explanatory Typologies in Qualitative Studies of International Politics." *International Organization* 59: 293–326.

Emery, Erin. November 1, 2002. "Senate District 3: Tapia, Lawrence Fighting for a Seat: Pueblo Lawmakers in a Tight Contest." *The Denver Post.*

Epstein, David, and S. O'Halloran. 1999. "A Social Science Approach to Race, Redistricting, and Representation." *American Political Science Review* 93: 187–91.

1999. "Measuring the Electoral and Policy Impact of Majority-Minority Voting Districts." *American Journal of Political Science* 43: 367–95.

Erickson, Robert, Gerald Wright, and John McIver. 1993. *Statehouse Democracy: Public Opinion and Policy in the American States.* Cambridge: Cambridge University Press.

Erie, Steven. 1988. *Rainbow's End: Irish Americans and the Dilemmas of Urban Machine Politics, 1840–1985.* Berkeley, CA: University of California Press.

Espino, Rodolfo. 2003. "Cross-Cutting Loyalties and Minority Representation in Congress: Racial, Ideological, or Geographic?" Paper presented at the Annual Meeting of the American Political Science Association, Philadelphia, Pennsylvania.

Estrada, Leo F. 2000. "Making the Voting Rights Act Relevant to the New Demographics of America: A Response to Farrell and Johnson." *North Carolina Law Review* 79: 1283–300.

Falcón, Angelo. 1988. "Black and Latino Politics in New York City." In *Latinos in the Political System,* ed. F. Chris García. South Bend, NC: Notre Dame University Press.

Fenno, Richard. 1978. *Home Style: House Members in Their Districts.* Boston: Little Brown.

2003. *Going Home: Black Representatives and Their Constituencies.* Chicago: University of Chicago Press.

Ferguson, Lew. September 14, 1998. "Kansas Governor's Race: A Study in Contrast." *Topeka Capital-Journal.*

Fine, Howard. November 17, 2003. "Loyal Opposition." *Los Angeles Business Journal.*

Fiorina, Morris P. 1994. "Divided Government in the American States-a by-Product of Legislative Professionalism." *American Political Science Review* 88(2): 304–16.

1999. "Further Evidence of the Partisan Consequences of Legislative Professionalism." *American Journal of Political Science* 43(3): 974–7.

Fiorina, Morris P., S. Abrams, and J. Pope. 2005. *Culture War? The Myth of a Polarized America.* New York: Longman.

Fitzgerald, Barbara. January 20, 2002. "After a Slow Climb, Hispanics Gather Power." *The New York Times.*

Fowler, Linda. 1992. "A Comment on Competition and Careers." In Limiting Legislative Terms, eds. Gerald Benjamin and Michael Malbin. Washington, DC: Congressional Quarterly Press.

Fowler, Linda, and R. McClure. 1990. *Political Ambition: Who Decides to Run for Office?* New Haven, CT: Yale University Press.

Fraga, Luis R., and David L. Leal. 2004. "Playing the 'Latino Card': Race, Ethnicity, and National Party Politics." *DuBois Review* 1: 297–317.

Fraga, Luis R., and Sharon Navarro. 2004. "Latinas in Latino Politics." Paper presented at 2004 State of the Discipline Latino Politics Conference, Texas A&M University, College Station, Texas.

Francis, Wayne, and L. Kenney. 1997. "Equilibrium Projections of the Consequences of Term Limits upon Expected Tenure, Institutional Turnout, and Membership Experience." *Journal of Politics* 59: 240–52.

2000. *Up the Political Ladder*. Thousand Oaks, CA: Sage.

Frymer, Paul. 1999. *Uneasy Alliances: Race and Party Competition in America*. Princeton, NJ: Princeton University Press.

Gaddie, R. Keith. 2004. *Born to Run*. Lanham, MD: Rowman and Littlefield Press.

Galant, Debra. March 9, 1997. "In Person: The Healing Professions." *The New York Times*.

Gallegos, Gilbert. July 8, 2002. "GOP Hopes to Upset Vigil-Giron." *Albuquerque Tribune*.

April 25, 2004. "Bush Advisers Wooing Hispanic Vote in N.M." *Albuquerque Tribune*.

Gann, L. H., and Peter J. Duignan. 1986. *The Hispanics in the United States: A History*. Boulder, CO: Westview Press.

Gay, Claudine. 2001. *The Effect of Minority Districts and Minority Representation on Political Participation in California*. San Francisco, CA: Public Policy Institute of California.

2006. "Seeing Difference: The Effect of Economic Disparity on Black Attitudes Toward Latinos." *American Journal of Political Science* 50: 4.

Gerber, Elisabeth R., R. Morton, and T. Rietz. 1998. "Minority Representation in Multimember Districts." *American Political Science Review* 92: 127–44.

Gerring, John. 2001. *Social Science Methodology: A Criterial Framework*. Cambridge: Cambridge University Press.

Glazer, Nathan. 1998. *We Are All Multiculturalists Now*. Cambridge, MA: Harvard University Press.

Goertz, Gary. 2006. *Social Science Concepts: A User's Guide*. Princeton, NJ: Princeton University Press.

González-Baker, Susan. 1999. "Su Voto Es Su Voz: Latino Political Empowerment and the Immigration Challenge." *Politics and Political Science*: September 1999 (American Political Science Association).

Griffin, John D., and Brian Newman. 2008. *Minority Report: Evaluating Political Equality in America*. Chicago: University of Chicago Press.

Grofman, Bernard, and L. Handley. 1989. "Minority Population Proportion and the Black and Hispanic Congressional Success in the 1970s and 1980s." *American Politics Quarterly* 17: 436–45.

Grofman, Bernard, and Chandler Davidson, eds. 1992. *Controversies in Minority Voting: The Voting Rights Act in Perspective*. Washington, DC: The Brookings Institution.

Hall, Richard L. 1996. *Participation in Congress*. New Haven, CT: Yale University Press.

Handley, Lisa. 2001. "Voting Patterns by Race/Ethnicity in Arizona Congressional and Legislative Elections, 1996–2000." Obtained via http://www.azredistricting.org

Harris, Fredrick. 1999. *Something Within: Religion in African American Political Activism*. New York: Oxford University Press.

Hastings, Maribel. May 10, 2001. "Los Latinos determinaran el diseño de muchos Distritos electorales." *La Opinión*.

Hayden, Bill. October 6, 2003. "Exhibit Celebrates Latinos in Delaware." *The News Journal*.

Haynie, Kerry L. 2001. *African-American Legislators in the American States*. New York: Columbia University Press.

Hero, Rodney E. 1992. *Latinos and the U.S. Political System: Two-Tiered Pluralism*. Philadelphia: Temple University Press.

Hero, Rodney E., and Caroline J. Tolbert. 1995. "Latinos and Substantive Representation In the U.S. House of Representatives: Direct, Indirect, or Nonexistent?" *American Journal of Political Science* 39: 640–52.

——— 1996. "A Racial/Ethnic Diversity Interpretation of Politics and Policy in the States of the U.S." *American Journal of Political Science* 40: 851–71.

Hochschild, Jennifer. 1998. *Facing Up to the American Dream*. Princeton, NJ: Princeton University Press.

Huckfeldt, Robert, and James Sprague. 1987. "Networks in Context: The Social Flow of Political Information." *American Political Science Review* 12: 1197–1216.

Jacobson, Gary C. 1997. *The Politics of Congressional Elections*. New York: Longman.

Jacobson, Gary C., and S. Kernell. 1981. *Strategy and Choice in Congressional Elections*. New Haven, CT: Yale University Press.

Johnson, James B., and Philip E. Secret. 1996. "Focus and Style Representational Roles of Congressional Black and Hispanic Caucus Members." *Journal of Black Studies* 26: 245–73.

Johnson, Malcolm. April 2, 2001. "New Senator Sees Himself as Role Model. *Associated Press*.

Jones-Correa, Michael. 1998. *Between Two Nations: The Political Predicament of Latinos in New York City*. Ithaca, NY: Cornell University Press.

Jones-Correa, Michael, and David L. Leal. 1996. "Becoming Hispanic: Secondary PanEthnic Identification Among Latin American-Origin Populations in the United States." *Hispanic Journal of Behavioral Sciences* 18(2): 214–54.

Kathlene, Lyn. 1994. "Power and Influence in State Legislative Policymaking: The Interaction of Gender and Position in Committee Hearing Debates." *American Political Science Review* 88: 560–76.

Kaufmann, Karen M. 2003. "Cracks in the Rainbow: Group Commonality as a Basis For Latino and African- American Political Coalitions." *Political Research Quarterly* 56(2): 199–210.

Kazee, Thomas. 1994. *Who Runs for Congress? Ambition, Context, and Candidate Emergence*. Washington, DC: Congressional Quarterly Press.

Kenyon, Charity. August 2001. "Senator Deborah Ortiz Fights for Community Issues." *Sacramento Lawyer*.

Kerr, Brinck, and Will Miller. 1997. "Latino Representation, It's Direct and Indirect." *American Journal of Political Science* 41: 1066–71.

Kessinger, Sarah. February 12, 2003. "Kansas Commerce Leader Pushes for Cuban Market." *The Hays Daily News*.

Key, V. O. 1984. *Southern Politics in State and Nation.* Knoxville, TN: University of Tennessee Press.

Kilson, Martin. 2002. "The State of Black American Politics." *Black Commentator. com.* http://www.blackcommentator.com/9_nul.html

Kim, Patty. October 30, 2000. "The Many Roads of the Campaign Trail." *The Oracle.*

Knoll, Benjamin R. 2009. "Amigo de la Raza? Re-Examining Determinants of Latino Support in the U.S. Congress." *Social Science Quarterly* 90(1): 176–92.

Kousser, J. Morgan. 1992. "The Voting Rights Act and the Two Reconstructions." In *Controversies in Minority Voting: A Twenty-Five-Year Perspective on the Voting Rights Act of 1965*, eds. C. Davidson and B. Grofman. Washington, DC: Brookings Press.

Kurland, Shannah. Spring 2001. "Brown Power vs. Black Power." *ColorLines.*

Latino National Political Survey. 1990. Inter-Consortium for Political and Social Research. University of Michigan.

Lazarsfeld, Paul F. and A. Barton. 1951. "Qualitative Measurement in the Social Sciences: Classification, Typologies, and Indices." In *The Policy Sciences: Recent Developments in Scope and Method*, eds. Daniel Lerner and Harold D. Lasswell, 155–92. Stanford: Stanford University Press.

Leal, David L. 2007. "Latino Public Opinion: Does It Exist?" In *Latino Politics: Identity, Mobilization, and Representation*, eds. Rodolfo Espino, David L. Leal, and Kenneth J. Meier. Charlottesville, VA: University of Virginia Press

Lengell, Sean. n.d. "Experience Needed Most in House, Foes Say." *Tampa Tribune.*

Liebschutz, Sarah. 1998. *Bargaining Under Federalism: Contemporary New York.* Albany, NY: State University of New York Press.

Loboguerrero, Cristina. April 26, 2004. "Hispanos son Clave en Comicios." *El Diario.*

Lublin, David Ian. 1997. "Congressional District Demographic and Political Data," American University, Washington, DC.

1997. *The Paradox of Representation: Racial Gerrymandering and Minority Interests in Congress.* Princeton, NJ: Princeton University Press.

1999. "Racial Redistricting and African-American Representation: A Critique of 'Do Majority-Minority Districts Maximize Substantive Black Representation in Congress?'" *American Political Science Review* 93: 183–6.

Lucas, Greg. November 17, 2000. "Squeaker of State Senate Race Appears Over: Democrat Mike Machado Likely Winner in San Joaquin Valley." *San Francisco Chronicle.*

Maestas, Cherie, L. Maisel, and W. Stone. 1999. "Stepping Up or Stopping? Candidate Emergence among State Legislators." Paper presented at the Southwestern Political Science Association Meeting, San Antonio, Texas.

Maisel, L. Sandy, and W. Stone. 1997. "Determinants of Candidate Emergence in U.S. House Elections: An Exploratory Study." *Legislative Studies Quarterly* 22: 79–96.

Mann, Christopher, and A. Gillespie. 2004. "Redistricting in a Multi-Racial Context: Majority-Minority Districts and the Maximization of Substantive

Representation For Blacks and Hispanics in Congress." Paper presented at the Midwest Political Science Association Meeting, Chicago, Illinois.

Mansbridge, Jane. 1999. "Should Blacks Represent Blacks and Women Represent Women? A Contingent Yes." *Journal of Politics* 61: 628–57.

Massey, Douglas, and N. Denton. 1993. *American Apartheid: Segregation and the Making of The Underclass*. Cambridge, MA: Harvard University Press.

Mayhew, David R. 1974. *Congress: The Electoral Connection*. New Haven, CT: Yale University Press.

McCarty, Nolan M. 2005. NOMINATE Roll Call Data for Colorado, New Jersey, and Texas.

McCarty, Nolan M., K. Poole, and H. Rosenthal. 2007. *Polarized America: The Dance of Ideology and Unequal Riches*. Cambridge, MA: MIT Press.

McClain, Paula et al. 2006. "Racial Distancing in a Southern City: Latino Immigrants' Views of Black Americans." *Journal of Politics* 68(3): 571–84.

McClain, Paula D., and A. Karnig. 1990. "Black and Hispanic Socioeconomic and Political Competition." *American Political Science Review* 84(2): 535–45.

McClain, Paula D., and S.C. Tauber. 1998. "Black and Latino Socioeconomic and Political Competition: Has a Decade Made a Difference?" *American Politics Quarterly* 26(2): 237–52.

McDaniel, Eric L. 2008. *Politics in the Pews: The Political Mobilization of Black Churches*. Ann Arbor, MI: University of Michigan Press.

McDonald, Michael P., and Samuel L. Popkin. 2001. The Myth of the Vanishing Voter." *American Political Science Review* 95: 963–74.

McElhenny, John. May-June 2003. "Climbing the Hill." *Harvard Magazine*. "Meddlesome Maes Has Own Agenda." March 19, 2003. *Albuquerque Tribune*.

Meier, Kenneth J., Paula McClain, et al. 2004. "Divided or Together? Conflict Cooperation between African-Americans and Latinos." *Political Research Quarterly* 57(3): 399–409.

Meier, Kenneth J., and Joseph Stewart, Jr. 1991. "Cooperation and Conflict in Multiracial School Districts." *Journal of Politics* 53(4): 1123–33.

Meinke, Scott R., and Edward B. Hasecke. 2003. "Term Limits, Professionalization, and Partisan Control in U.S. State Legislatures." *Journal of Politics* 65(3): 898–908.

Miller, Warren, and Donald Stokes. 1963. "Constituency Influence in Congress." *American Political Science Review* 57: 45–56.

Minta, Michael D. 2009. "Legislative Oversight and the Substantive Representation of Black and Latino Interests in Congress." *Legislative Studies Quarterly* 34: 193–218.

Moncrief, Gary, R. Niemi, and L. Powell. 2004. "Time, Term Limits, and Turnover: Trends in Membership Stability in U.S. State Legislatures." *Legislative Studies Quarterly* 29: 357–81.

Moncrief, Gary, P. Squire, and M. Jewell. 2000. *Who Runs for the Legislature*. Upper Saddle River, NJ: Prentice Hall.

Moncrief, Gary, J. Thompson, and W. Cassie. 1996. "Revisiting the State of U.S. State Legislative Research" *Legislative Studies Quarterly* 21: 301–35.

Montejano, David. 1999. *Anglos and Mexicans in the Making of Texas, 1836–1986*. Austin, TX: The University of Texas Press.

Morehouse, Sarah M., and M. E. Jewell. 2004. "States as Laboratories: A Reprise." *Annual Review Political Science* 7: 177–203.

Murphy, Brian P. May 22, 2002. "Passaic Dems Stand by Girgenti While Hispanic Leaders Search for Senate Seat." Obtained via http://www.politicsnj.com

National Hispanic Leadership Agenda Congressional Scorecard. 2001. 105th Congress. National Association of Latino Elected and Appointed Officials (NALEO). Available via http://www.naleo.org

Nechemias, Carol. 1987. "Changes in the Election of Women to U.S. State Legislative Seats." *Legislative Studies Quarterly* 12: 125–42.

Nelson, Albert. 1991. *Emerging Influentials in State Legislatures*. New York: Praeger.

Ngai, Amy. 2006. "Instant Incumbents." *Gotham Gazette*. http://www.gotham-gazette.com/print/1775

Nickens, Tom. June 14, 1999. "Parties Courting Hispanic Vote." *St. Petersburg Times*.

Niemi, Richard, and L. Winsky. 1987. "Membership Turnover in U.S. State Legislatures: Trends and Effects of Districting." *Legislative Studies Quarterly* 19: 49–59.

Oppenheimer, Bruce. 2005. "Deep Red and Blue Congressional Districts: The Causes and Consequences of Declining Party Competitiveness." In *Congress Reconsidered* (8th ed.), eds. Lawrence Dodd and Bruce Oppenheimer, 135–58. Washington: Congressional Quarterly Press.

Pantoja, Adrián, and G. Segura. 2003. "Does Ethnicity Matter? Descriptive Representation in Legislatures and Political Alienation Among Latinos." *Social Science Quarterly* 84: 441–60.

Pendleton, Scott. March 16, 1994. "Inspired by 'Superstar' Congressman, Hispanic Republicans Run for Office." *Christian Science Monitor*.

Petracca, Mark. 1992. "Predisposed to Oppose: Political Scientists & Term Limitations." *Polity* 24: 657–72.

Phillips, Anne. 1998. "Democracy and Representation: Or Why Should It Matter Who Our Representatives Are?" In *Feminism and Politics*, ed. A. Phillips, 224–40. New York: Oxford University Press.

1995. *The Politics of Presence*. Oxford: Clarendon Press.

Pinderhughes, Dianne. 1987. *Race and Ethnicity in Chicago Politics: A Reexamination of Pluralist Theory*. Chicago: University of Illinois Press.

Pitkin, Hanna. 1967. *The Concept of Representation*. Berkeley, CA: University of California Press.

Poole, Keith T., and Howard Rosenthal. 1996. *Congress: A Political-Economic History of Roll Call Voting*. New York: Oxford University Press.

Porter, Eduardo. April 4, 2001. "GOP to Help Hispanics Seek Greater Representation." *The Wall Street Journal*.

Portes, Alejandro. 1984. "The Rise of Ethnicity: Determinants of Ethnic Perceptions among Cuban Exiles in Miami." *American Sociological Review* 49: 383–97.

Preuhs, Robert R., and Rodney E. Hero. 2009. "A Different Kind of Representation: Black and Latino Descriptive Representation and the Role of Ideological Cuing." *Political Research Quarterly* (forthcoming).

Propp, Wren. March 17, 2004. "Six Seeking Seat Vacated by Coll." *Albuquerque Journal.*

Ragin, Charles. 1999. *Fuzzy Set Social Science.* Chicago: University of Chicago Press.

Rauh, Grace. February 20, 2004. "From Assembly to Senate – Manny Diaz Looks to Make the Jump." *Mountain View Voice.*

Rice, David. December 13, 2002. "Hispanic Legislators May Be Pacesetters." *Winston-Salem Journal.*

Richardson, Lilliard, and P. Freeman. 1995. "Gender Differences in Constituency Service Among State Legislators." *Political Research Quarterly* 48: 169–79.

Riddlesperger, James W. 2003. "Redistricting in Texas." Paper presented at the 2003 Meeting of The Southern Political Science Association, New Orleans, LA.

Rodríguez, Clara. 1987. *Puerto Ricans: Born in the U.S.A.* Boulder, CO: Westview Press.

Rogers, Reuel. 2006. *Afro-Caribbean Immigrants and the Politics of Incorporation.* Cambridge: Cambridge University Press.

Rojas, Aurelio. February 22, 2003. "GOP Goal: Appeal to Minorities." *Sacramento Bee.*

Roper, Peter. December 23, 2002. "State Senator-Elect to be a Major Player for Pueblo in the Statehouse." *The Pueblo Chieftain.*

Santos, Adolfo, and J. Huerta. 2001. "An Analysis of Descriptive and Substantive Latino Representation in Congress," In *Representation of Minorities in the United States: Implications for the 21st Century,* ed. Charles E. Menifield. Lanham, MD: University Press of America.

Schmidt Sr., Ronald, Barvosa-Carter, Edwina, and Torres, Rodolfo. 2000. "Latina/o Identities: Social Diversity and US Politics." *PS: Political Science and Politics* 33(3): 563–7.

Sears, David O. et al. 2000. *Racialized Politics: The Debate About Racism in America.* Chicago: University of Chicago Press.

Selby, W. Gardner. December 4, 2003. "Valley Demo Won't Try for D.C. Post." *San Antonio Express-News.*

Skerry, Peter. 1993. *Mexican Americans: The Ambivalent Minority.* Cambridge, MA: Harvard University Press.

Soloway, Mara. October 16, 2003. "Church Service Jump-Started Civic Career." *Houston Chronicle.*

Squire, Peverill. 1992. "Legislative Professionalization and Membership Diversity in State Legislatures." *Legislative Studies Quarterly* 17(1): 69–79.

2007. "Measuring Legislative Professionalism: The Squire Index Revisited." *State Politics and Policy Quarterly* 7: 211–27.

Stein, Letitia. April 27, 2003. "John Quiñónes: A Rising Star in GOP Ranks." *The Orlando Sentinel.*

Steller, Tim. 2000. "Two Open Seats Create Potential for Horse Race." *Arizona Daily Star.*

Stewart, Joseph. January 31, 2003. "Competitiveness Analysis for Adopted and Alternative Congressional District Plans in Arizona." Obtained via http://www.azredistricting.org

Stiles, Laura. October 9, 2002. "Goglas, Ramos Tackle Issues in Sixth AD Race." *Suffolk Life Newspapers.*

Stinchcombe, Arthur L. 1968. *Constructing Social Theories.* New York: Harcourt Brace.

Stonecash, Jeffrey M. 1993. "The Pursuit and Retention of Legislative Office in New York, 1870–1990: Reconsidering Sources of Change." *Polity* 26: 301–15.

Stout, David. February 28, 1995. "A First for the Assembly." *The New York Times.*

St. Petersburg Times. October 20, 2000. "Henriquez for State House 58." Editorial.

Swain, Carol M. 1993. *Black Faces, Black Interests: The Representation of African-Americans in Congress.* Cambridge, MA: Harvard University Press.

Swers, Michele. 2001. "Are Congresswomen More Likely to Vote for Women's Issue Bills Than Their Male Colleagues?" In *American Politics: Cases and Readings.* 2nd Ed., ed. Karen O'Connor, 159–65. New York: Longman Publishers.

Sylvester, Sherry. April 22, 2002. "Hispanic Newcomers in Pivotal District 125 Race." *San Antonio Express News.*

Tampa Tribune. October 17, 2002. "Bob Henriquez in House District 58." Editorial.

Tate, Katherine. 1999. "African-Americans and Their Representatives in Congress: Does Race Matter?" Center for the Study of Democracy, UC Irvine Working Paper.

2004. *Black Faces in the Mirror.* Princeton, NJ: Princeton University Press.

Terrell, Steve. April 20, 2004. "At Forum, Senate Hopefuls Focus on Issues and Manners." *Santa Fe New Mexican.*

September 4, 2002. "Letitia Montoya to Challenge Roman Maes in 2004." *Santa Fe New Mexican.*

Theriault, Sean M. 2009. *Party Polarization in Congress.* Cambridge: Cambridge University Press.

Thomas, Ken. March 5, 2004. "Democrats, GOP to Compete for Hispanic, Swing Voters." *Contra Costa Times.*

Thomas, Sue, and J. Welch. 1991. "The Impact of Gender on Activities and Priorities of State Legislators." *Western Political Quarterly* 44: 445–56.

Tien, Charles. 2009. "Review Essay: African American and Hispanic Representation: Theory and Evidence." *Polity* 41: 267–77.

Uhlaner, Carole Jean, and F. Chris García. 2002. "Latino Public Opinion." In *Understanding Public Opinion,* 2nd ed., ed. Barbara Norrander and Clyde Wilcox, 77–101. Washington, DC: Congressional Quarterly Press.

UTA Magazine. Winter 2001. "Rep. Elvira Reyna." Obtained via http://utamagazine.uta.edu

Vaca, Nicolás. 2004. *The Presumed Alliance.* New York: HarperCollins Publishers.

Van Evera, Stephen. 1997. *Guide to Methods for Students of Political Science.* Ithaca, NY: Cornell University Press.

Verba, Sidney, K. Schlozman, and H. Brady. 1995. *Voice and Equality: Civic Voluntarism in American Politics.* Cambridge, MA: Harvard University Press.

Vigil, Maurilio. 1996. *Hispanics in Congress: A Historical and Political Survey.* Lanham, MD: University Press of America.

Villareal, Roberto E., and Norma G. Hernandez (eds). 1991. *Latinos and Political Coalitions: Political Empowerment for the 1990s.* New York: Greenwood Press.

Wallison, Ethan, and John Mercurio. April 23, 2001. "Caucus' Move Could Limit Hispanic Gains." *Roll Call.*

Weideman, Paul. August 4, 2002. "Profile: Roman Maes." *Santa Fe New Mexican.*

Weiss, Peter. June 4, 2003. "Big Win For Glenn." Obtained via http://www.nj.com

Weissberg, Robert. 1978. "Collective and Dyadic Representation in Congress." *American Political Science Review* 72: 535–47.

Welch, Susan. 1990. "The Impact of At-Large Elections on Black and Hispanic Representation." *Journal of Politics* 52: 1050–76.

Welch, Susan, and John Hibbing. 1984. "Hispanic Representation in the US Congress." *Social Science Quarterly* 65: 328–35.

Whitby, Kenny. 1997. *The Color of Representation.* Ann Arbor, MI: University of Michigan Press.

Worrall, J., and Pratt, T. 2004."Estimation Issues Associated with Time-Series – Cross-Section Analysis in Criminology." *Western Criminology Review* 5.

Wright, Gerald. 2004. "Ideology Party Identification Data." Obtained via http://mypage.iu.edu/~wright1

Young, Iris Marion. 1997. "Deferring Group Representation." In *Ethnicity and Group Rights. Nomos 39. Yearbook of the American Society for Political and Legal Philosophy*, eds. Ian Shapiro and Will Kymlicka, 249–76. New York: NYU Press.

Index

abortion, 14, 129
African American Effect, 130
African-American majority districts
  election of African-American legislators
    and, 3, 80t, 80–1
  election of Latino legislators and, 72–4
African-Americans
  biracial coalitions and, 26, 55, 98, 104,
    140, 143
  black churches and, 110, 122–3
  California election success and, 65
  as Congressional representatives, 19,
    57, 127
  Democratic Party and, 4–5, 25–6, 51–2,
    90, 143–4
  district composition and election of,
    80–1, 142
  elected in non African-American
    majority districts, 77, 80–1
  election of Latinos and, 16, 51–2, 59, 71,
    73–4, 88–93, 104, 140, 143
  elections with two minority candidates
    and, 86–7
  empowered by African-Americans in
    positions of authority, 120
  in lower vs. upper chambers, 59–60
  in majority combination with Latinos,
    77–8, 80, 82, 93–5, 95t, 98,
    101, 104
  as legislators promoting African-
    American interests, 74
  literature on race and representation
    and, 22–6, 34, 36, 128

majority African-American districts
  and, 3, 80–1
multi-candidate primaries and, 98, 101
New Jersey and, 72–3, 135–6
Poole-Rosenthal scores and, 132–135,
  135t
racial discrimination and, 3, 9, 104–5
redistricting and, 77–8, 82, 95–6,
  142
representing Latinos and, 73–4,
  118–19, 140
sixty-five percent rule and, 62–3
substantive representation and, 26–7,
  132–3, 137
support for larger government
  and, 14–15
tension with Latino community,
  71–2, 96
trust of African-American legislators
  and, 29, 108
Voting Rights Act and, 52, 54, 81
vs. Latino candidates, 3, 95–6, 104,
  111–12, 144
vs. Latinos as largest minority group,
  19–20
Aguilar, Ray, 87t, 87–8, 90t
Aguilera, John, 99t, 99–100, 119–20
Aldarondo, David, 110, 119, 145–6
Álvarez, Manny, 99, 99t
American Community Survey, 42
anti-communism, 7, 145–6
Apodaca, Tom, 89–90
Archer, Bruce, 102